CW00602433

THE **Michael's**

BRUSSELS & ANTWERP

Managing Editor
Michael Shichor

Series Editor
Amir Shichor

INBAL TRAVEL INFORMATION LTD.

Inbal Travel Information Ltd.
P.O.Box 1870 Ramat Gan 52117
Israel

Intl. ISBN 965-288-116-3

Graphic design: Michel Opatowski
Cover design: Bill Stone
Photography: Daniel Mordzinski
Photo editor: Claudio Nutkiewicz
Editorial: Sharona Johan, Or Rinat, Lisa Stone
D.T.P.: Irit Bahalul
Printed by Havatzelet Press Ltd.

Sales in the UK and Europe:
Kuperard (London) Ltd.
9 Hampstead West
224 Iverson Road
London NW6 2HL

Distribution in the UK and Europe:
Bailey Distribution Ltd.
Learoyd Road
New Romney
Kent TN28 8X

U.K. ISBN 1-85733-098-6

CONTENTS

ANTWERP

TABLE OF MAPS

Preface

Belgium is a tiny country, packed with exciting cosmopolitan cities, beautiful architecture, and a wealth of art treasures. It is a gourmet's delight and a shoppers' paradise.

Brussels is not only the capital of Belgium, but also in many ways the capital of Europe, and the headquarters for NATO, the EEC and many international organizations and companies. The free spirit of the city is symbolised by the Manneken-Pis statue, and the citizens certainly know how to enjoy life. The Grand' Place and Hôtel de Ville at the heart of the city have witnessed many historic events and the tradition continues with all sorts of activities taking place here, like the stately Ommegang pageant. Architectural and artistic masterpieces abound and there are no less than 100 museums.

Antwerp too has its share of architectural gems, most notably the Gothic Cathedral of Our Lady, and the Town Hall. You can wander through old alleyways and narrow streets, explore Rubens' House and the treasures of the Museum of Fine Arts. The zoo, in the heart of town, provides a restful oasis of greenery where you can see reptiles, dolphins and creatures you have never seen before. Antwerp is also the place to look at diamonds, even if you do not wish to buy.

Linda White, a travel correspondent in Europe, explored Brussels and Antwerp, planning the tour routes which lead you through these beautiful cities, and collected essential updated material on shopping options and a wide range of entertainment. The staff at Inbal researched, compiled and edited the Guide.

Our aim is to give you a good understanding of Brussels and Antwerp, to lead you to the best and most exciting attractions and to ensure that you derive maximum pleasure from your trip. We are sure that the effort invested in compiling this guide will be justified by your enhanced enjoyment.

Michael Shichor

Using this Guide

In order to reap maximum benefit from the information in this guide, we advise the traveller to carefully read the following advice. The facts contained in this book were compiled to help the tourist find his or her way around and to ensure that he enjoys his stay to the upmost.

The Introduction will supply you with details which will help you make the early decisions and arrangements for your trip. We advise you to carefully review the material, so that you will be more organized and set for your visit. Upon arrival in Brussels and Antwerp, you will already feel familiar and comfortable, more so than otherwise would have been the case.

The basic guideline in all "MICHAEL'S GUIDE" publications is to survey places in a primarily geographical sequence. The detailed introductory chapters discuss general topics and specific aspects of getting organized. The tour routes, laid out geographically, lead the visitor up and down the city's streets, providing a survey of the sites and calling attention to all those details which deepen one's familiarity with Brussels and Antwerp, and make a visit there so much more enjoyable.

Since Brussels and Antwerp are highly esteemed for their cuisine, wines, shopping and entertainment, we have devoted a special chapter to "Making the Most of your Stay" in each city. Here you will find a broad range of possibilities to suit your budget, which will help you enjoy your stay.

A concise list of "musts" follows, describing those sites without which your visit is not complete.

The reader will notice that certain facts tend to recur. This is deliberate; it enables the tourist who starts out from a point other than the one we choose, to be no less informed. The result is flexibility in personal planning.

The rich collection of maps covers the tour routes and special attractions in great detail. They were especially prepared for this book, and will certainly add to the efficiency and pleasure of your exploration of Brussels and Antwerp.

A short chapter is provided on shopping, restaurants, and the other essences of each city. These will help visitors fill their suitcases and stomachs – comprehensively, thoroughly, and as economically as possible. Here again, a broad spectrum of possibilities is provided.

To further facilitate the use of this guide, we have included a detailed index. It includes all the major sites mentioned throughout the book. Consult the index to find something by name and it will refer you to the place where it is mentioned in greatest detail.

Because times and cities are dynamic, an important rule of thumb when travelling, and especially when visiting cities like Brussels and Antwerp, should be to consult local sources of information. Tourists are liable to encounter certain inaccuracies in this guide, and for this we apologize.

The producer of a guide of this type assumes a great responsibility: that of presenting the right information in a way which allows for an easy, safe and economical visit. For this purpose, we have included a short questionnaire and will be most grateful for those who will take the time to complete it and send it to us.

Have a pleasant and exciting trip – Bon Voyage!

PART ONE – A TASTE OF WHAT'S TO COME

Belgium became an independent kingdom in 1831. It has been fought over and occupied by the Spanish, the Austrians, the French and the Dutch. Situated between France and Holland, Germany and England, it is one of the smallest countries in Europe, yet it is densely populated and highly industrialised.

The northern Flemish part of the country is very different in language, culture and outlook from the southern Walloon part. The division of the country makes a delightful contrast. Anyone who thinks Belgium is a flat, dull country has not strayed far from its well-lit expressways; there are grand castles tucked away behind villages which seem to have come straight out of a Breughel painting; abbeys which are noted for their strong, dark beers, and carillons (organs) which are famous for their clarity. Belgium boasts one of the best cuisines of Europe, and the Belgians claim that a two-star restaurant in France would only get one star here.

There are countless folklore events throughout the year in almost every town and city. They range from simple village fairs to music and art festivals, trade fairs, sports events, and the most spectacular of all, the Ommegang pageant in Brussels' Grand' Place.

Because it has so much packed into such a small space, Belgium is an easy country to visit. Its two main cities, Brussels and Antwerp, are less than an hour's drive apart, yet very different in atmosphere. Brussels is the capital, a bilingual and cosmopolitan city, famous for its museums, galleries, elegant shops and its superb cuisine. Antwerp is the chief commercial center of Belgium, an international center of the diamond business and a thriving port, which also has wonderful art galleries, interesting museums and magnificent churches.

History

Belgium derives its name from Gallia Belgica, the ancient Roman name for the southern part of the Low Countries – an area which was chiefly populated by tribes of Celtic origin. This area was conquered by Julius Caesar in the first century, and roads that were built in Roman times have remained important routes to this day.

A Germanic element was added to the Celtic population when the Franks started moving into this area in the third century. Their migration was more or less halted by the forests of Flanders and Brabant and by the defensive frontier of the Roman Empire. The Franks thus settled mostly in the northern part of the Low Countries, and are now roughly represented in Belgium by the Flemish element. The Walloons of the southern area of Belgium are in general descendants of the Celtic people, with a strong Latin influence.

This area (Belgica) was the cradle of the Frankish Carolingian dynasty, and part of Charlemagne's great empire. However, after his death in 814AD this unity was shattered. Most of the region was made part of Lotharingia, later Lower Lorraine. In medieval times, Belgium was broken up into feudal duchies such as Brabant, Luxembourg, Flanders, Hainaut, Limburg and Liege. In the 15th century the area of present day Belgium passed to the dukes of Burgundy and then to the Hapsburgs.

Political division of the area into Holland and Belgium took

An example of the lovely work shown at the Plantin-Moretus Museum in Antwerp

place when the northern provinces of the Low Countries won their independence from Spain in 1609. Belgium was annexed by France in 1797, but was handed to the Netherlands by the Treaty of Paris in 1815. In 1815 Belgium was made part of the Netherlands, but resentment of Dutch rule led to rebellion, and an independent state was declared in 1831. Under King Leopold I and Leopold II the country made rapid progress. Industrialization and colonization of the Congo brought great prosperity.

Belgium was internationally recognised as a "perpetually neutral" state in 1838, but in both World Wars Germany violated this neutrality and occupied the country. During the years of occupation, property was confiscated, people were deported, the economy was disrupted and major battles were fought on Belgian soil.

Following the war, King Leopold III, who had surrendered the country unconditionally to the Germans in 1940, was freed, but he was not welcome in Belgium and stayed in exile until 1950. In 1951 he abdicated in favor of his son Baudouin.

Belgium, the Netherlands and Luxembourg formed the Benelux Union in exile in 1944, to remove trades and customs barriers. Post-war recovery was rapid, but crises

Well preserved uniforms and paintings decorate Brussels' Army and Military History Museum

arising from long-standing tensions between Flemish and French speaking elements toppled several Belgian governments in the 1960s. Independence was granted to the Congo (now Zaire) in 1960. A constitutional reform in 1971 created three partly autonomous regions (Flanders, Wallonia and Brussels), but ethnic discord has continued.

Modern Brussels has become a major international center. The city is host to many European and international organisations. The most important is the North Atlantic Treaty Organisation (NATO).

There has been some opposi-

An Antwerpian scene

tion to NATO using Belguim as a base, especially for nuclear missiles, and in 1984 there was a series of bomb attacks directed against NATO-connected targets.

Brussels is also a center for many European organisations such as the European Economic Community (EEC), European Coal and Steel Community, and the European Atomic Energy Community. In addition, many international business corporations make Brussels their European headquarters.

Standing in the shade at the Parc de Bruxelles

Brussels is a cosmopolitan city and an important cultural and artistic center.

Geography

Belgium is one of the smallest countries in Europe, with an area of 11,780 square miles. It is bounded by the Netherlands on the north and northeast, by West Germany and Luxembourg on the east and southeast, by France on the south and west, and to the northwest has a 40 mile coastline on the North Sea. North

Belgium is flat. Major battles of the First World War were fought on the beaches there. This part of the country contains many historic cities as well as great artistic and architectural treasures. South Belgium is quite different, consisting mostly of the beautiful Ardennes mountains, which rise to approximately 3,300 feet. Belgium is crossed by the Scheldt and the Meuse rivers and their tributaries. The Scheldt flows into an estuary on the North Sea, and the Meuse flows into the Netherlands and then into the North Sea. The country is crossed by a dense network of canals.

Economy

The country has a dense network of rail, road and water transport, which facilitates the import of raw materials and the export of finished products. Belgium is a leading shipping nation, and the economy depends on exports.

The main agricultural activities are dairying, cattle raising, and growing cereal crops. The emphasis in industry is on heavy industries such as steel, chemicals and petrochemicals, but there are also sugar refineries and food processing plants. Leather goods, glass, pottery and bricks are also manufactured and traditional industries such as textiles, printing, and diamond cutting continue to thrive.

Population and Language

Belgium has a population of approximately 10 million people. Although Julius Caesar said that of all the Gauls the *Belgae* were the bravest, their descendants say that there are no Belgians and that one is either Flemish or Walloon. Ethnic feelings run deep, and have been bitter, but efforts are being made to overcome the problem.

The visitor to Belgium will notice the division primarily in the language spoken. French is the language of Wallonia in the south, while Flemish, a dialect of Dutch, is spoken in Flanders in the north. Officially, the country is bilingual, but the language border cuts the country almost exactly in half, north and south, with Brussels – the capital – claimed by both sides. The people in the

A relief at the Musée de la Ville de Bruxelles

Flemish part of the country generally speak better English than those in the Wallonia regions. Tourists are advised to speak English rather than French in the Flemish regions, or to inquire politely if French is spoken in that area.

Many towns have both French and Flemish names, which can be confusing. If, for instance, you are driving to Liège and are suddenly confronted with a highway sign pointing to Liuk, remember they are one and the same (see "Practical Tips – Towns with Two Names").

Art

Architecture

The oldest buildings surviving intact in Belgium are Romanesque, dating from the 11th and 12th centuries. These are either Meuse-Romanesque or Scheldt-Romanesque; the former are simpler and the latter more ornate.

The **Gothic** period (13th-16th centuries) produced a number of cathedrals, churches and civic buildings. The buildings

Exquisitely stained glass at the Brussels' Bourse

Brussels in miniature – a display at the Museé de la Ville de Bruxelles

are characterised by pointed spires, broken and cross-ribbed arches, and supporting outer buttresses. The outer supporting structure took the weight of the building and allowed the builders to create impressive interiors. The Gothic buildings became increasingly high and lavishly ornate. In Brussels, **Cathedrale Saint Michel**, with its remarkable stained glass windows, and **Notre-Dame du Sablon**, are two outstanding examples of Gothic architecture. The **Antwerp Cathedral** is a fine example of the later more flamboyant Gothic style. It was in the Gothic period that the guilds acquired great wealth and power, and it was they who built many fine buildings, such as the **Hôtel de Ville** (Town Hall) in Brussels.

The **Renaissance** period (it came late to Belgium, mid 16th-17th centuries), unlike the Gothic period, was restrained and the style emphasized the horizontal rather than the vertical. **Antwerp's Town Hall** is a fine example of this style, with a façade nearly 300 feet long. In domestic architecture, brick and stone began to replace wood, but the typical pitched roofs, gables and windows with leaded panes were still used.

The **baroque** period (17th century) was grandiose, using a variety of rich decoration, exaggeration, contrasts, and distortions. This seems to be partly related to a Catholic reaction against the restrained Protestant styles. The **Church of St. Carolus Borromeus** in Antwerp (1615-21) is a baroque Jesuit style church. Baroque façades were often added on to Romanesque or Gothic buildings.

In the 18th century the baroque

style was replaced by the lighter and less grandiose style influenced by the French rococo. In the late 18th century there was a drastic change in architecture, and neoclassicism became fashionable, characterised by severe, symmetrical and dignified form and design.

The most interesting development in the 19th century was **art nouveau**, of which **Victor Horta** was a leading exponent. His house in Brussels is now a museum, and there are many buildings which exemplify this style. The style used asymmetry, rich textures and decoration inspired by organic forms (see "Musée Horta").

Twentieth century architecture is largely characterized by huge, uniform blocks of buildings, but in Brussels there is still considerable variety and style in the houses and public buildings.

Painting

Painting flourished in Flanders, under the patronage of wealthy men, and many artists of the Flemish school were not actually born in Flanders, but came to work here. **Jan van Eyck** was outstanding in the 15th century. His work displays brilliant clear coloring, realism and acute observation of nature. His skill as an oil painter made him and his school famous, and the Italian humanist Bartolomeo Fazio called him "the prince of painters of our age". Van Eyck worked for Philip the Good, Duke of Burgundy, who considered him irreplaceable, and sent him on diplomatic missions. His observation of natural light and atmospheric conditions was far superior to his predecessors.

Van Eyck painted altarpieces and also illuminations for a *Book of Hours* (now in the Museum of Ancient Art in

Turin). One of his most celebrated paintings is *The Arnolfini Wedding* (National Gallery, London). All the objects in the painting have symbolic meaning; the little dog represents fidelity, the clogs cast aside show that the couple stand on holy ground, the peaches represent fertility. The interior illumination brings out the contrasting textures of velvet, beads and fabric. Jan van Eyck was one of the first, and one of the greatest, painters of independent portraits – a new art-form in the 15th century.

Other 15th century Flemish artists are the Master of Flémalle, Robert Campin, who was the first to paint life-size figures, Roger van der Weyden, whose works can be seen in Brussels and Antwerp, Van der Goes, Dirk Bouts and Hans Memling (or Memlinc). Van der Weyden turned away from the quiet calm compositions of Van Eyck in favor of more emotional works. In 1435 he was appointed official painter to the city of Brussels, and he held the post for 30 years. Gerard David introduced subjects from everyday life to painting, which he portrayed with human warmth, and Quentin Metsys (Massys) developed the style further, using a more realistic proportion between the figures and the background. At about this time, landscape painting began to develop, and can be seen in the work of Joachim Patinir.

Hieronymous Bosch was a unique artist who lived from 1450-1516. His work is full of complex symbols and indicates an inexhaustible imagination. His most famous painting is *The Garden of Delights* (Museo del Prado, Madrid), in which an imaginary, almost surrealistic world is depicted. In a fantastical landscape, hundreds of naked figures emerge or are half hidden in giant eggs, shells, floral forms, glass domes and cylinders. Some ride animals and play erotic games. Nothing explicitly sexual is depicted but the symbols and poses are clearly erotic, the figures are daintily drawn and brightly illuminated in pale colors. Some have seen in Bosch's work an expression of ideas later formulated in the doctrine of predestination;

others see in his vision an inner world of dream symbols which makes Bosch a forerunner of the surrealist school which emerged in the 20th century.

In the early 16th century Italy blossomed as the center of the High Renaissance, and art and architecture expressed a new vision of human grandeur and heroic action. Artists such as Leonardo da Vinci, Michelangelo, Bramante and Raphael attracted artists from all over Western Europe, who came to Florence and Rome to learn from these men of genius. Although the High Renaissance lasted only about 25 years, the artists of this time set the standards and norms in European art for at least three centuries.

Jan Gossaert (Mabuse) was one of the Flemish artists who visited Italy in the High Renaissance period, and on his return he introduced nude figures and mythological subjects into his painting – as seen for instance in *Venus and Cupid* (Musées Royaux des Beaux-Arts). In Gossaert's *Agony in the Garden* (Staatliche Museen, Berlin), he shows his talent for creating effects of light and space, which he probably learnt from studying Italian painters, particularly Mantegna. Other artists who were influenced by the Italian Masters are Jan Metsys, Frans Floris and Martin de Vos, who had worked in Tintoretto's studio. These artists were, however, more followers than leaders, and Flemish artists expressed a

One of Jordaens' masterpieces in the Museum of Fine Arts in Antwerp

At the Musée de la Ville de Bruxelles

more original spirit in their portrait painting. Among the best Flemish portrait painters were Adrien Key, who worked in Antwerp, and Pieter Pourbus who worked in Bruges. Another original trend in early 16th century Flemish art was an increasing sensitivity to the moods of nature.

The most outstanding Flemish artist of the 16th century was **Pieter Breughel the Elder** (1525-69). He too traveled to Italy, but he did not adopt the nude or mythological figures; instead the influence of the Italian Masters is felt in the monumental harmony of form and space which characterises his work. This can be seen in his *Landscape with the Fall of Icarus* (Musées Royaux des Beaux-Arts, Brussels). Icarus himself is an insignificant figure – only his legs are visible as he plunges into the water while a farmer ploughs his field and a shepherd tends his flock, both concerned with more down to earth matters. Breughel's *Triumph of Death* (Museo del Prado, Madrid) is a frightening panorama of human mortality, somewhat reminiscent of Bosch's *Garden of Delights*. Probably one of his most popular paintings is *Harvesters* (Metropolitan Museum of Art, New York), which shows peasants in the midday heat working, eating and sleeping. For Breughel the peasants typify a fatalistic acceptance of man's bondage to earth and the seasons. His *Hunters in the Snow* (Kunsthistoriches Museum, Vienna) shows weary hunters plodding through the snow. The landscape is peaceful and the figures closely observed. Breughel does not sentimentalize the peasants, but shows their simple humanity, and his land-scapes are expansive and dignified. He seems to accept fate with stoicism and peace.

The glory of Flemish painting in the 17th century is dominated by a single extraordinary painter, **Peter Paul Rubens** (1577-1640). His authority and influence in Flanders was like that of Michelangelo in Central Italy in the 16th century, or that of Bernini in contemporary Italy. Rubens was born in Cologne, had an excellent education in Latin and theology, and spoke and wrote six languages. He was probably the most learned artist of all time. He traveled widely, and through diplomatic service he established contacts with kings and princes throughout Western Europe. His house in Antwerp has been restored (see "A Glimpse of a Golden Age – Grote Markt to Rubens' House") and was in fact a factory where a steady stream of monumental works was produced by Rubens and his assistants. The door was made twenty feet high to allow panels and canvases to be carried out. Rubens charged in proportion to his personal participation in a work. Most paintings were designed by him, and assistants then executed the paintings from color sketches that he made. Rubens would then add the final touches.

A brightly colored maritime design atop the Steen, one of Antwerp's ancient castles

Rubens first visited Italy in 1600 and studied Roman sculpture and the artists of the High and Late Renaissance: Leonardo da Vinci, Raphael, Michelangelo, Correggio, Titian, Tintoretto, Veronese, Caracci and Caravaggio. Heroic figures feature strongly in Rubens' work, which is characterised by tremendous physical energy. In the Cathedral in Antwerp one can see Rubens' *Raising of the Cross* (part of a triptych), in which muscular figures reminiscent of Michelangelo tug and push the Cross upward, forming a mass of struggling figures. This work exemplifies the energy and drama of baroque art. In *Rape of the Daughters of Leucippus* and, even more so, in *Fall of the Damned* (both in Alte Pinakothek, Munich) Rubens' power reaches a climax, with an outpouring of energy and drama, rich colors and textures, and contrasts of light and dark. Rubens was commissioned to

Rubens' House in Antwerp

work for Maria de Medici, dowager queen of France, and when she was later driven out of France and took refuge in Flanders, Rubens helped support her.

Rubens' work can be seen at Musées Royaux des Beaux-Arts in Brussels, the Museum voor Schone Kunsten (Fine Arts) in Antwerp, the Cathedral in Antwerp and Rubens' House in Antwerp.

Anthony van Dyck (1599-1641) was once an assistant to Rubens, and later worked independently as a friendly rival. He lived in Flanders, Italy and England, and was already an accomplished painter in his late teens. The broad movement of color and light in his pictures seems to show the influence of Rubens, but van Dyck's individuality is evident in his light, graceful figures, the sensitive expressions of his figures, and their aristocratic refinement. Van Dyck was employed by King Charles I of England, and painted his portrait. Although his portrait subjects have dignity, they never seem posed or artificial. Van Dyck set the tone for such official portraits in England for more than a century.

Jacob Jordaens (1593-1678) was strongly influenced by Rubens but was more excessive; his colors are stronger, contrasts more violent, and the overall effect exaggerated. His *Allegory of Fecundity* is nevertheless regarded as a masterpiece of Flemish baroque art, and can be seen with many other of his works in the Musées Royaux des Beaux-Arts, Brussels.

Frans Snyders, Paul de Vos, Jan Fyt, David Teniers the Younger and Adriaen Brouwer

Marching through the streets of Brussels

painted genre, landscape and animal paintings with faithful observation and sense of color. Cornelis de Vos was a distinguished portrait painter.

By the end of the 17th century, Flemish painting was past its prime, and it was not until the 19th century that a revival took place. After about 1830 many Flemish artists were influenced by the French Romantic school. Romanticism focused on the terror, the majesty and the unknowable forces in nature. It was a movement affecting literature, music and opera as well as painting. It had a strong emotional element, and emotion took precedence over intellect, content over form, color over line and intuition over judgement.

Antoine Wiertz (1806-65) was a Romantic painter who executed vast compositions of mythological, religious or moral subjects. His paintings are often macabre and sensational. There is a museum devoted to his work in Brussels.

In the 19th century Flemish art was also influenced by a study of Dutch art, and depicted daily life and leisure activities rather than grand religious or mythological subjects. Edouard Agneessens is known for his portraits, Joseph Stevens for his animal paintings, Alfred Stevens for his portraits of elegant ladies, and Constantin Meunier for paintings of workers in town and country.

Towards the end of the 19th century, a number of artists in Brussels, Oslo and Vienna developed a radical new approach to painting, where direct emotional expression took precedence over aesthetics; form, figures and colors were all distorted in order to convey emotion more powerfully. **James Ensor** (1860-1949) did some early work in Impressionist style, but soon abandoned the method and started working with shocking and unexpected themes and violently contrasting strong colors and shapes. His development as an artist seems to parallel that of Van Gogh, though he was apparently unaware of his existence. Ensor's painting *The Entry of Christ into Brussels in 1889* can be seen in the Museum voor Schone Kunsten, Antwerp. Christ himself is barely noticeable and seems a powerless figure in a hostile crowd of figures wearing ugly, frightening and evil masks. The painting shocked Ensor's contemporaries, and even the group of radical artists, *The Twenty*, to which he belonged, refused to exhibit the painting. Ensor's approach is similar to that of Norwegian Edvard Munch (1863-1944), and both of them were influential in the development of the German Expressionist movement in the early 20th century. Other Belgian expressionists were G. de Smet (1877-1943) and Constant Permeke.

In the 20th century, the surrealist painter **René Magritte** (1898-1967) stands out. Surrealism was initially a literary movement which rejected logic and used the unconscious for creative purposes. This dream world sometimes took on a nightmare character, and can be either fantastic or terrifying and disturbing. René Magritte expresses the lighter side of surrealism – his work is witty and fascinating, never sinister. He depicts absurdities in everyday life; double images, opaque objects becoming transparent and people and things becoming transformed. Paul Delvaux is another Belgian surrealist, and works of both artists are exhibited in the Musée Royaux des Beaux-Arts (modern section) in Brussels.

Sculpture

The oldest sculptures in Belgium date back to the 11th century. They can be seen in churches and museums and one example is the bronze font of St. Barthelemy in Liege.

At the end of the 14th and beginning of the 15th cen-

At St. Paul's Church in Antwerp

turies, two Netherlands sculptors, Claus Sluter and Claus de Werwe, were highly influential in Northern Europe. They were brought to Dijon by the Dukes of Burgundy. Claus Sluter's vigorous sculptures are imbued with drama and emotion, and the figures are naturalistic and individual. Unfortunately, much of the work of this school of sculptors in Belgium was destroyed or damaged, mainly by 16th century iconoclasts.

In the 15th century, wood carving developed in order to supply altarpieces and panels for churches. By the 16th century, sculptors were working in Renaissance style – Jean Mone, Lancelot Blondeel, Jacques Du Broeucq, Pieter Coecke and Cornelis Floris.

The baroque sculptors include Jérôme Duquesnoy the Elder, who sculpted the famous Manneken-Pis in Brussels, his sons Francois and Jérôme the Younger, Luc Fayd'herbe and Artus Quellin the Elder. Their work consisted mostly of furnishings and ornamentation for churches. Jean de Cour (1627-1707) who worked in Liege studied with Bernini who was the undisputed leader of Roman High baroque, and one of the most influential artists of the 17th century.

In the 19th century, **Constantin Meunier**, who was also a painter, produced some sculptures in which the subject matter was not religious but rather everyday figures of people, particularly workers. His works can be seen in the Musées Royaux des Beaux-Arts and the museum in his own name in Brussels. Other 19th century sculptors are Van Geel, Van Hool, Rik Wouters and **Jef Lambeaux**. Lambeaux created the *Brabo Fountain* in

Brabo Fountain, in Antwerp's Grote Markt

the Grote Markt (see "The Flavor of Old Antwerp – Around Grote Markt and the Cathedral"), and his sculptures can also be seen in the Hansa House in Antwerp.

Metro Art

Art in Brussels has gone underground – literally. The city's Metro is more than a public transportation system; it has become a modern art museum. Forty-eight Belgian artists have created works at as many stations, ranging from sculpture to painting.

The idea of making art accessible to the people of Brussels was formed almost at the start of construction of the Metro in 1964. Five years later, when the first line opened, a commission for art in the Metro was set up, and in 1976, the first art work appeared. Since then, the idea has been refined, so that now the architect and artist work together on the concept of a station from the very beginning.

The Comte de Flandre station is entirely suspended, like a cathedral, the perfect setting for artist Paul Van Hoeydonck's *16 x Icarus*. Bronze figures in homage to astronauts are suspended from the ceiling over the tracks. Van Hoeydonck has even "exhibited" on the moon: his work *Fallen Astronaut* was taken on the Apollo 15 mission in 1971 and left on the moon.

The walls of this station are of blue stone from the Belgian town Hainaut. Its color varies, depending on whether or not polished stones were used. The stations are built of marble and other stone, which is expensive material, but it more than pays for itself by saving cleaning and repair costs.

At the Hankar station, Roger

Somville applied 300 kilos (more than 600 pounds) of paint directly on the wall for his huge mural *Notre Temps* (Our Times).

It took Somville and his students two years to complete the mural, sometimes working suspended above the tracks as the trains rushed by underneath. The signature includes the names of all the students who helped with the project. All the faces in the painting are Somville's face, and the work progresses from right to left, from bad to good as the artist saw it.

Some of the works are alongside the tracks, so they can be seen from the trains or examined closely while one waits. Others are at the station entrance or on upper levels.

The variety of art provides for almost every taste, but one that is universally popular is *La Grande Taupe et le Petit Peintre*, by Paul de Gobert, at the Vandervelde station; a mural depicting the four seasons in the nearby Valley of the Woluwe. One side of the tracks shows the valley in the morning and the other, in the afternoon. Close attention reveals such details as spider webs and even fossils.

Brochures containing station maps and suggested art itineraries are available. A book, *L'Art dans le Métro*, which contains color photographs and information about each work and artist (with English translations at the back), can be found in local book shops or at the S.T.I.B. office, Avenue de la Toison d'Or 20, in the Galerie Toison d'Or shopping arcade, the 6th floor. Tel. 515.30.64.

PART TWO – SETTING OUT

How to Get to Belgium

BY AIR
Belgium's principal international airport is at Brussels (Zaventem) and the national airline is *Sabena*, which flies to 53 countries. Some 60 airlines serve Brussels. The airport is 14 km from the city, and there are rail, bus and taxi services to Brussels. There are also local flights to other cities in Belgium.

Antwerp has an international airport at Deurne, 6 km from the city center. It is served by 21 airlines, and there are bus connections to the Central Railway Station, the city center and also Brussels airport. Charleroi and Liege also have international airports.

BY FERRY
There are ferry connections for cars and passengers between Southend and Oostende, Hull and Zeebrugge, and also ferries which link Dover, Folkestone and Felixtowe with Oostende and Zeebrugge.

BY TRAIN
Brussels has 5 large railway stations, three of which have international connections, the busiest being the North and South stations. Antwerp's Central Station also has international connections.

BY CAR
The expressways in Belgium are excellent, with international connections in all directions. Public transport within the country is very well developed and convenient.

Crossing Borders
Border crossing formalities are seldom stringent and are sometimes nonexistent. Some small roads at the border with the Netherlands are totally unmanned and even expressway crossings may not require stops.

Documents and Customs

Visitors to Belgium from European Economic Community countries, Canada and the U.S.A. do not require visas. Visitors from other countries should check with their local Belgian consulate.

Travelers may bring in the following duty-free: 100 cigarettes or 25 cigars, 1.5 litres of spirits or five litres of wine – or a total value of up to 7,000 francs.

Insurance

Health insurance and insurance against theft or loss of your belongings is strongly recommended in order to assure that you enjoy your holiday with peace of mind. Inclusive insurance can usually be arranged through a travel agent.

When to Come; National Holidays

There is plenty to see and do at any time of the year, but the ideal time to visit is in summer between June and September, when the days are warm and the nights are cool. Rain falls in summer as well as winter, so at any time of year you will need an umbrella. The winters are very cold and wet.

Public Holidays in Belgium

January 1 – New Year's Day
May 1 – Labor Day
July 21 – National Day
August 15 – Assumption Day
November 1 – All Saints' Day
November 11 – Armistice Day
December 25 – Christmas Day

Holidays without fixed dates are Easter Monday, Ascension Day (around May) and Whit Thursday (around March-

April). If holidays fall on Sunday, the following Monday is a holiday. There are no city holidays in Brussels.

In addition to the national public holidays, Antwerp has a few of its own:

January 2
May 8 – Liberation Day
July 11 – Flemish National Day
November 15 – Day of the Belgian Royal Dynasty
December 26 – Boxing Day

How Much will it Cost?

Brussels and Antwerp are generally considered as expensive cities in Europe, but perhaps less so than Paris. The most expensive part of one's stay is accommodation, and this each visitor can determine according to personal circumstances and

Cheers!

requirements (see "Accommodation). It is worth checking whether weekend discounts are available, because unlike many other cities, hotels in Brussels often have cheaper rates on weekends.

Eating out is generally a rather expensive pleasure, but if you order *plate du jour* (fixed price menu), the price is considerably less. Taxis cost approximately 90 francs to

start and an additional 40 francs per kilometer, but public transport is extensive and efficient and not very expensive. Entertainment is not especially expensive, and the entrance fee to museums varies; most cost approximately 100 francs but some do not charge for admission at all.

Tourists should remember that they are entitled to a tax refund on their purchases, provided they spend at least 7,001 francs in one shop. Tax varies on different types of goods, and may be up to 25% on luxury items. Thus a leather coat or other expensive items may actually be quite reasonable if you buy them tax-free (see "VAT").

The EEC Building

Practical Tips for Getting Around

Currency

There is no limit on amounts of currency that can be taken into or out of the country. The currency is the Belgian franc; there are half franc, one franc, five franc and 20 franc coins, and notes of 50, 100, 500, 1000 and 5000 francs. Belgian francs can be used in Luxembourg, but Luxembourg francs are not accepted in Belgium.

VAT

The tax on goods in Belgium ranges from 6 to 25 percent. The country's Value Added Tax rebate plan for tourists is not as well publicized as plans in other countries are, but such a plan does exist. The refund is applicable only to items costing 7,001 francs or more. Most major stores give the refunds. A form must be filled out at the time of purchase. The store will stamp the form, and the customs agent will stamp it again at the border when the buyer shows the unused goods. Mail the form to the shop and the refund will be sent on to you.

Measurement, Electricity and Time

Belgium uses the metric system for measuring. The following information will help you make conversions.

WEIGHT
28.35 grams – 1 ounce
453 grams – 1 pound
1 kilogram – 2.2 pounds

VOLUME
0.47 liters – 1 pint
1 liter – approximately 1 quart
3.79 liters – 1 gallon

DISTANCE
2.54 centimeters – 1 inch
30.5 centimeters – 1 foot
1 meter – approximately 1 yard
1 kilometer – 0.628 miles
1.6 kilometers – 1 mile

As in the rest of Europe, what would be the American first floor is called the ground floor, and the next one up is the first floor.

Belgium time is G.M.T+1. The country goes on Daylight Savings Time on the last Sunday of March. Savings Time ends the last Sunday of September. The 24-hour clock is more commonly used than am and pm. 13:00 hours is 1pm, 24:00 hours is midnight.

The electricity voltage used is 220; visitors from America will need transformers for electrical appliances and visitors from Great Britain will need plug adaptors. Many hotels provide these.

Towns with Two Names

Here is a list of those confusing towns with two names. The local usage is given first, the alternative beside it (whether French-Flemish or Flemish-French). Not all are in Belgium; note that Aachen is just within the German border, but is important as a directional marker on highway signs.

LOCAL VERSION/ ALTERNATIVE VERSION
Aachen/ Aix-la-Chappelle
Antwerpen/ Anvers Brainel/

Alleud Eigenbrakel
Braine-le-Chateau/ Kasteel-brakel
Brugge/ Bruges
Bruxelles/ Brussels
Gent/ Gand
Liege /Luik, Luttig
Lier/ Lierre
Mechelen/ Malines
Mesen/ Messines
Namur/ Namen
Oostende/ Ostende
Rijssel/ Lille
Tournai/ Doornik

In the flower market at Brussels

BRUSSELS

Brussels epitomises Europe at its sophisticated best. Brussels is typified by the Grand' Place, great art in museums and in the Metro, lace and chocolates, good food, flower markets, and the Manneken-Pis. It is frequently called the capital of Europe because it is the headquarters of NATO and the European Community (EC), and the seat of the General Secretariat of the Benelux Nations. Some 20,000 diplomats live here in three diplomatic corps – one to the king, one to NATO and one to the EEC.

The city is also headquarters for some 500 international organizations and about 1200 multinational companies. It is Europe's third convention center after London and Paris.

Brussels is a hybrid, claimed by both Flanders and Wallonia. Although most residents of Brussels speak French, Brussels is situated in the Flemish part of the country, which has sometimes led to conflict. Both Flemish and French are spoken, and signs are in both languages. The city has practically adopted English as its third language. Foreigners account for almost a quarter of the population of one million.

From the elegant 15th-century Hôtel de Ville (Town Hall) to the imposing glass skyscrapers, Brussels' architecture reflects an attachment to the material side of life. The *Bruxellois* enjoy their festivals, both religious (they are staunchly Catholic) and secular. The city is at its best during the medieval pomp and pageantry of Ommegang, held on the first Thursday in July. This historic and aristocratic pageant has its origins in the 14th century.

The people take their food and drink seriously, too, and it is not without reason that a prime restaurant district is known as the *Ilot Sacré* – Sacred Island. Coffee and beer are popular drinks, served at sidewalk cafés when the weather is fine, or beside the fireplace of a cozy pub on the more frequent grey days.

Brussels is a great place to visit at any time of year. The visitor may enjoy the glorious parks and squares when it is sunny or take refuge from the

In a Brussels cocktail bar

rain in one of the hundred museums, in more than a dozen shopping arcades, or even in the Metro, which has become the most accessible of art galleries.

In short, visitors there on business will find many pleasures, and visitors there for pleasure will find plenty to keep them busy.

History

The name of the city probably derives from the word *Bruocsella*, meaning village of the marsh, as there was an extensive marsh here before the river Senne was canalized. The first inhabitants of the area were Gallo-Romans who took refuge here when harried by the Franks, after the withdrawal of the Romans.

The Franks were the next settlers, arriving in the area in the seventh century. Brussels was a crossing place on the route between Cologne and Ghent and Bruges. The village grew into a town, with a market in the area now occupied by the Grand' Place. The Counts of Louvain (and later the Dukes of Brabant) settled on the higher ground in the south-east of the city (Coudenberg).

During the 12th, 13th and 14th centuries, Brussels was a center for manufacturing luxury fabrics for export, and an economic and political center. New city walls were built in the 14th century. These walls were reinforced in the 16th century and stood until the 19th century, but they have been replaced by ring boulevards around the city, and today the only remnant of the walls is Porte de Hal.

In the early 15th century, Brussels prospered and became an important trade center for lace, tapestry, jewellery and church furniture. In 1430 Brussels became the seat of the Dukes of Burgundy, and in 1477 seat of the governors of the Spanish Netherlands. In the Burgundian period, Brussels gained political and artistic prestige. The beautiful Hôtel de Ville (Town Hall) was built in the first half of the 15th century as were many Gothic churches and cathedrals.

In St. Michel Cathedral, which was built in the 15th century

Philip II of Spain transferred the government of the Netherlands from Mechelin to Brussels in the late 16th century, but the Spanish governors met with enormous opposition to the reactionary measures of Philip against the growing number of protestants, which culminated in insurrection and the execution of the Netherlands' leaders Egmont and Horn in the Grand' Place.

The rule of Archdukes Albert and Isabella (1598-1621) ushered in a period in which art and architecture flourished. This peaceful time came to an end in the War of the Grand Alliance against France, in which Brussels was heavily bombarded in 1695. The city was seriously damaged, especially around the Grand' Place.

After the War of the Spanish Succession, Belgium came under the control of the Austrian Hapsburgs. In 1714 Brussels became the seat of the governors of Austrian Netherlands. There was strong opposition to their rule, and in 1717 Frans Anneessens, leader of the city guilds, was beheaded in the Grand' Place for defending the privileges of Brussels against the encroachment of the Austrians.

In 1746 Brussels was occupied for a short time by the French,

Marionettes in the Toone

but was soon restored to Austria. The latter half of the 18th century was a period of prosperity for Brussels; Palais du Roi was built, partly on the site of the old Coudenberg Palace which had burnt down, Palais de la Nation and Place Royale were also built.

In 1792 war broke out between Austria and France, Belgium was annexed by France, and Brussels was reduced to chief town of the French department of the Dyle. At the turn of the century, Napoleon broke down the city walls and replaced them with boulevards. In 1815 the Battle of Waterloo changed the fate of Belgium once again. Belgium was made part of the United Kingdom of the Netherlands, and for a time Brussels became the royal residence of William of Orange-Nassau. The Belgians resented Dutch dominance, and in 1830 revolution broke out in Brussels. Brussels was proclaimed the capital of newly independent Belgium, although William held out in the citadel of Antwerp until he was forced to admit defeat in 1839.

Modernisation of the city began in the 19th century. In 1835 Europe's first passenger rail service was opened between Brussels and Mechelen. The river Senne was covered, slums were cleared, roads were improved, road tolls abolished (1860), Palais de Justice was built, and great expansion took place.

Although Belgium was internationally recognised as neutral in 1838, the country was invaded and the German army marched into Brussels in August 1914. Adolphe Max, burgomaster of the city, set an example of passive resistance, and was deported for refusing to cooperate with the Germans.

An underground newspaper was printed in Brussels during the war and much heroic resistance was displayed by the Belgians in spite of danger. Edith Cavell, the English nurse, was shot here in 1915 for helping fugitive soldiers escape to Holland.

After World War I, neutrality was abolished and Belguim signed a military convention with France in 1920. However, when the Rhineland was occupied by Germany in 1936, Belguim refused to accept French and British troops or hold staff talks. In May 1940 the country was again attacked by Germany. French and British troops then moved in, but Brussels was taken by the Germans. King Leopold III surrendered. The Belgian people resisted heroically and were of great help to the Allies. The occupation lasted until liberation began in September 1944, with the Allies reaching Brussels on September 3 1944.

Hitler launched a counter-attack on December 16, into the Ardennes. The area was liberated in the Battle of the Bulge and by January 1945 the Germans were out of Belgium.

In post-war years, Brussels has expanded and been modernised. The World Fair was held here in 1958, and in the 1960's Brussels became the base for the European Economic Community and The North Atlantic Treaty Organisation (NATO). The city has expanded tremendously and many foreign residents have settled in the city. Wealthier inhabitants live in luxurious houses in the suburbs, and skyscrapers abound in the city center.

Besides being a national capital and metropolis, Brussels is also an internation-

The building of the EEC headquarters

al business and political center, and an industrial and banking center too. Many American and multinational companies have their European head offices in Brussels.

Brussels has a Free University which has French and Flemish speaking divisions, plus the royal academies of science, medicine, French and Flemish language and literature, and countless museums. The Palais des Beaux-Arts is a major cultural center for art, music, films, theater and literature.

How to Get There

BY AIR

About 60 airlines serve Brussels and there are direct flights from most major European cities. Sabena (Belgian Airlines) flies to 78 destinations in 53 countries including 27 in Africa, more than any other airline. It is the only major airline serving Togo, Nigeria and Angola.

Brussels airport is only nine miles from the city, and there is a train station below the arrival hall which is linked with the North and Central Railway Stations in town. The ride to the North Station takes 15 minutes, to the Central Station, 20 minutes. Trains depart about every half hour from about 6am to about midnight. The ticket and information counter is open daily 8am-9pm; tickets can be purchased on the trains, but a sizeable supplement is charged, so it is best to buy your ticket at the station.

After midnight, there is a bus service into the city. A number of hotels provide limousine service, including the *Metro-*

Color-originality on a painted tram

pole, *Hyatt*, *Sheraton*, *Ramada*, *Novotel*, *Sofitel*, *Fimotel*, *Belson* and *Chambord*.

Sabena buses connect the Brussels airport with Ghent, Antwerp and Liege. Trains connect the airport with a number of cities. The trip to Antwerp takes about 30 minutes; to Ghent, about 45 minutes; to Namur, 50 minutes; to Bruges, 55 minutes; to Liege, 65 minutes; and to Ostende and the coast, 75 minutes.

Airport baggage carts are available for a fee; put the coins in the slot. A machine changes 100 francs. Leave the cart near the exit for a partial refund.

BY TRAIN

The Belgian railway network is the densest in the world. Five large stations serve Brussels, and three offer connections on international trains, though international service at the Central Station is limited. Most of the international service is at the North (Bruxelles-Nord/Brussel-Noord) and South (Midi/Zuid) stations. The Leopold station is near the EEC, and the car-train station is Schaerbeek. In addition, Congrés/Kongres and Chapelle/Kapellekerk Stations provide domestic service.

Inter-city and local trains fan out in all directions and for long trips, the Trans-Europe Express (TEE) and Trans-Europe Night (TEN) coaches link Brussels with Milan, Rome, Marseilles, Nice, Basel and other large cities. A boat train to Ostende provides service to Dover, England.

The Belgian rail system includes 13 inter-city (IC) and 16 InterRegional (IR) lines, plus local feeder lines

(L trains). The ICs depart hourly during the day to inland destinations. Trains to Cologne, Germany (3-3.5 hours away), Rotterdam (1-1.5 hours away) and Amsterdam (2 hours away), also depart hourly. Trains to Luxembourg depart every two hours. There are 12 trains daily to Paris (2.5 hours away). Night trains go to Copenhagen, Denmark; Frankfurt, Mainz and Munich in Germany; Basel and Zurich in Switzerland; Marseilles and Nice in France; and Milan, Italy.

The Central, North and Midi Stations have complete services: left-luggage, post offices, etc., but are closed for a few hours each night, from 1:30-4am.

Belgian trains are slightly more expensive than some others in Europe, but special and seasonal tickets are available. Inquire about prices and conditions of Tourrail, Network Season Tickets, Reduction Cards, weekend and day tickets to the coast or the Ardennes.

The railway timetable (*Indicateur/Spoorboekje*) has English explanations, but other information is in French and Flemish only. Watch out for schedule changes in spring and autumn and for reduced service on holidays.

Belgium is such a small country that the Belgian Railway (SNCB) operates no night service on inland routes, but the company does have sleepers and couchette cars on international routes. Diners, too, are attached only to international express trains, though some inland trains have mini bars or buffet cars.
(SNCB information: Tel. 219.26.40)

A TEE Club in the South Station can be found off the main concourse. It has a lounge for snacks and drinks, plus baths and showers. It is reserved for holders of TEE tickets, but properly dressed passengers are seldom denied entry.

Baggage must be checked in two hours before departure. An auto-on-train service operates seasonally to ski or beach resorts from the Schaerbeek Station. Bicycles can be rented at 48 Belgian stations.

BY CAR
Like the railways, the expressways are excellent – and they are well lit all the way. Belgium is so small and flat that it is possible to drive across the country in a couple of hours, but within the cities

Riding in a horse and cart by the arched buildings of the Grand' Place

(especially Brussels) heavy traffic slows one considerably. Ring roads are designed to make access to the cities smooth and long-distance driving easy, but in reality they can be confusing. In Brussels, inadequate directional markers and numerous detours can have one literally driving around in circles.

CAR-RENTAL

Car rental firms generally have automatic-transmission cars in stock, as well as sports cars, prestige cars, diesels and minibuses. Rentals can be picked up at the airport and main railway stations, or delivery can be made to hotels. Most of the firms accept credit cards.

The following are a few of the major car rental firms:

Avis: Place Rogier 3. Tel. 730.62.11, 720.09.44.
Autorent: St. Lazarusplaats 5. Tel. 217.15.50.
Budget: Ave. Louise 275A. Tel. 332.24.94, 720.80.50.
Hertz: Blvd. M. Lemonnier 8. Tel. 702.05.11, 720.60.44.

Fly/drive and rail/drive arrangements can be made through airlines, the railways or travel agencies.

Belgian drivers have the reputation of being among the most erratic in Europe, perhaps because road tests were not introduced until the 1970s. However, knowledge of the rules of the road will make driving easier for the visitor.

Seat belts are compulsory for anyone sitting in the front seats, and children under 12 must ride in the back seat.

Speed limits for cars and motorcycles are 60k.p.h. (37m.p.h.) in built-up areas, 120k.p.h. (75m.p.h.) on expressways and major highways, and 90k.p.h. (56m.p.h.) on other roads. In normal driving conditions, driving below 70k.p.h. (43m.p.h.) on expressways is forbidden. Special speed limits are denoted by round signs circled in red.

Roads are generally good, but driving conditions can be bad, and fog occurs rather frequently. Fog lights are required in heavy rain or when visibility is less than 100 meters (110 yards). Motor cyclists must use lights and helmets at all times. Ice may form on the roads in winter.

Watch out for bicycles – cycling is popular here and cycle paths often run beside roads. When turning, give way to traffic on the cycle paths as well as to pedestrians.

At intersections and in traffic circles, except when otherwise posted, traffic coming from the right (including bicycles and mopeds) has right of way. Trams always have right of way.

Visitors should have drivers' licenses from their home country or international drivers' licenses.

The penalties for driving under the influence of alcohol are severe. The police can demand a breath test and can confiscate the driver's license on the spot. In addition, fines range from 6000 to 60,000 Belgian francs and the driver can be jailed.

For minor traffic offenses, the police can collect on-the-spot fines of about 1500 Belgian francs. For more serious offenses (speeding, driving through red lights, crossing solid white lines), the fine is about 8000 francs.

Keep a red warning triangle in the car in case of breakdown. In such a case, place it 100 feet behind the car (330 feet on an expressway) and switch on the car's hazard-warning lights. In case of minor accidents, it is not obligatory to call the police unless the parties cannot agree on what happened. However, it

will help simplify insurance claims to fill in a European Accident Statement, available from the police.

Orange emergency phones are located at frequent intervals along expressways and major highways. From a regular phone, emergency service can be reached by dialing 112.

Automobile clubs offer information and breakdown services both to their own members and members of similar organizations in other countries. The major clubs are:

The Royal Automobile Club of Belgium (RACB): Rue d'Arlon 53. Brussels. Tel. 287.09.11.

Touring Club de Belgique (TCB): Av. Carton de Wiart 128. Tel. 233.22.11.

Vlaamse Toeristenbond (VTB): Blvd. E. Jacqmain 126, Brussels. Tel. 217.51.65.

In winter, information about road conditions is available day and night (tape-recorded nights and weekends) from the *RACB* Tel. 287.09.11, 8:30am-5pm, and from the *TCB* Tel. 233.22.361 9am-6pm, or Tel. 233.25.87, for a 24-hour service.

Finding parking on the street can be difficult, but Brussels has dozens of parking garages.

Public Transportation

Brussels' public transportation system is extensive and efficient, encompassing the Metro, pre-Metro, trams and buses. The pre-Metro is made up of underground trams serving stations that are ready to become part of the Metro system.

Stations are marked with a blue "M" on a white background. At present, the network covers 48 Metro stations, but expansion is progressing swiftly. Metro maps are available from the information offices at the Porte de

Namur, Rogier and Midi stations.

Single tickets can be used on all forms of transport and transfers are free. The tickets can be purchased at Metro entrances or from drivers of buses or trams.

Savings are available with a 24-hour ticket, good for unlimited travel during a 24-hour period. These tickets are sold at the tourist information offices. A 10-ride ticket can be purchased at Metro ticket offices and at some newsstands. A five-ride ticket is sold only on trams and buses. The last two must be punched at automatic machines at Metro entrances or near the front doors of buses and trams, otherwise they will not be considered valid.

Tram and bus stops are marked by red-white or blue-white signs. If a stop is marked *sur demande* (on demand) you must signal the driver to stop.

Public transport operates frequently from 6am to midnight, with less frequent service (usually hourly) from midnight to 6am.

Taxis in Brussels are expensive, but all are metered. Cost is approximately 90 francs to start and 40 francs per kilometer (60 francs/mile). At night a supplement is charged. The price of the ride includes service charge; just round the amount up for an extra tip. Chaufeured cars are available; ask the tourist office or check the yellow pages.

A crowd warming up with a little music at the Place du Grand Sablon

Accommodation

Hotel accommodation and services are at a very high standard in Brussels, with prices to match, yet less expensive than equivalent establishments in Paris, Rome, London or Amsterdam. It is possible to find comfortable lodging at moderate prices. Room reservations can be made, for a small fee, either at the Brussels Tourist Office (T.I.B.) or at the Tourism Center. T.I.B. in the Hôtel de Ville, Grand' Place. Tel. 513.89.40, fax 514.45.38. The Tourism Center is at Rue Marché-aux-Herbes 63. Tel. 504.03.90, fax 504.02.70. A free booking service, which reserves rooms throughout

Belgium, is available from the Belgian Tourist Reservation (BTR), Blvd. Anspach, 111, 1000, Brussels. Tel.(32-2) 513.74.84, fax (32-2) 513.92.77

Breakfast may be Continental and included in the price of the room, or buffet at extra cost. Some lower-priced hotels have rooms without private facilities.

Here is a listing of some of Brussels' recommended hotels.

LUXURY HOTELS

Sheraton-Brussels: Place Rogier 3. Tel. 224.31.11, fax 224.34.56. Location is not recommended for single women.

Hilton Brussels: Blvd. de Waterloo 38. Tel. 504.11.11, fax 504.21.11. Near the luxury shopping area.

Royal Windsor Hotel: Rue Duquesnoy 5. Tel. 505.55.55, fax 505.55.00. Situated near the Grand' Place.

FIRST-CLASS HOTELS

Amigo: Rue de l'Amigo 1-3. Tel. 547.47.47, fax 513.52.77. A lovely hotel just off the Grand' Place, still under family management. Large comfortable old style rooms.

Europa Brussels: Rue de la Loi 107. Tel. 230.13.33, fax

230.36.82. Situated near the EEC headquarters.

Royal Crown Hotel Brussels: Rue Royale 250. Tel. 220.66.11. fax 217.84.44.

Jolly Hotel Atlanta: Blvd. Adolph-Max 7. Tel. 217.01.20, fax 217.37.58. Near the center of town.

Mètropole: Place de Brouckère 31. Tel. 217.23.00, fax 218.02.20. Renovated to its former Art Nouveau splendor. Good choice for style and location.

VERY GOOD HOTELS

Arenberg: Rue d'Assaut 15. Tel. 511.07.70, fax 514.19.76. Central location.

Holiday Inn: *Brussels City Center*:Chaussée de Charleroi 38. Tel. 533.66.66. fax 538.90.14. A little far from the main tourist attractions in town.

Astoria: Rue Royale 103. Tel. 217.62.90. fax 217.11.50. An elegant hotel.

President World Trade Center: Blvd. Emile Jacqmain 180. Tel. 217.20.20, fax 218.82.02.

Archiméde: Rue Archiméde 22. Tel. 231.09.09, fax 230.33.71. No restaurant. Near the EEC headquarters.

Bedford Hotel Brussels: Rue du Midi 135. Tel. 512.78.40, fax 514.17.59.

Euro-flat: Blvd. Charlemagne 50. Tel. 230.00.10, fax 230.36.83. No restaurant. Near the EEC headquarters.

Diplomat: Rue Jean Stas 32. Tel. 537.42.50, fax 539.33.79. No restaurant.

Too beautiful to eat

COMFORTABLE HOTELS

Delta: Chaussée de Charleroi 17. Tel. 539.01.60, fax 537.90.11. Near the luxury shopping area.

Président Nord: Blvd. Adolphe-Max 107. Tel. 219.00.60, fax 218.12.69. No restaurant.

Président Centre: Rue Royale 160. Tel. 219.00.65, fax 218.09.10.
No restaurant.

MODERATE HOTELS

Chambord: Rue de Namur 82. Tel. 513.41.19. fax 514.08.47.
No restaurant.

Cascade: Rue de la Source 14. Tel. 538.88.30. fax 538.92.79.
No restaurant.

New Hotel Siru: Place Rogier 1. Tel. 217.75.80, fax 218.33.03.

Diplomat: Rue Jean Stas 32. Tel. 537.42.50, fax 539.33.79.
No restaurant.

Ibis Sainte-Catherine Brussels Centre: Rue Joseph Plateau 2. Tel. 513.76.20. fax 514.22.14.
No restaurant. Near the center of town.

YOUTH HOSTELS
The following youth hostels both have facilities and services far superior to those in the average youth hostel. They accept couples, and people of any age. Groups with guides are also accepted. Both hostels have inexpensive restaurants.

Auberge de Jeunesse Jacques Brel: Rue de la Sablonnière 30. Tel. 218.01.87. fax 410.39.05. An old building which has been restored. Showers in the rooms. Opened in November 1987. 120 beds.

Brueghel-IYHF: Heilige Geeststraat 2. Tel. 511.04.36. Near the Church of Notre-Dame de la Chapelle, where Pieter Brueghel is buried. New building with 100 beds.

Suburban Hotels

FIRST-CLASS
Mayfair: Ave. Louise 381. Tel. 649.98.00, fax 649.22.49.

Copthorne Stéphanie: Ave. Louise 91. Tel. 539.02.40, fax 538.03.07. Near the luxury shopping area.

VERY GOOD HOTELS
Alfa Chelton: Rue Veronése 48. Tel. 735.20.32, fax 735.07.66. No restaurant.

Belson: Chaussée de Louvain 805. Tel. 735.00.00, fax 735.60.43.

COMFORTABLE HOTELS
Brussels Président: Ave. Louise 315. Tel. 640.24.15, fax 647.34.63. No restaurant.

County House of Brussels: Square des Héros 2. Tel. 375.44.20, fax 375.31.22.

MODERATE HOTELS
Fimotel Expo: Ave. Impératrice Charlotte 6. Tel. 478.70.80, fax 478.10.00.

L'Agenda: Rue de Florence 6. Tel. 539.00.31. fax 539.00.63. Not far from the luxury shopping area.

Near the Airport

Some visitors will find it convenient to stay outside town, especially near the airport.

A FIRST CLASS HOTEL
Holiday Inn: Holidaystraat 7. Tel. 720.58.65, fax 720.41.45.

VERY GOOD HOTELS
Novotel: Olmenstraat 1. Tel. 725.30.50, fax 721.39.58.

Sofitel: Bessenveldstraat 15. Tel. 725.11.60, fax 721.43.45.

A MODERATE HOTEL
Fimotel Aéroport: Berkenlaan 5. Tel. 725.33.80, fax 725.38.10.

General Information

Tourist Services

Brussels and Belgium are well organized to answer visitors' questions. The Brussels Tourist Office (T.I.B.) is in the Hôtel de Ville (Town Hall) on the Grand' Place (Tel. 513.89.40, fax 514.45.38). The Office of Tourism for French-Speaking Belgium and Flemish Belgium is at Rue Marché-aux-Herbes 63 (Tel. 504.03.90, fax 504.02.70).

The **T.I.B.** can provide listings of restaurants, hotels, museums and other practical brochures; a "tourist passport" for Brussels offering many reductions and other advantages; tour guides speaking 14 languages; multilingual hostesses for fairs, exhibitions and congresses; press and promotional services; a weekly program of cultural events known as the *BBB Agenda*; reservations for shows and concerts (by phone for members of TELETIB – see "Entertainment"); cassette guides of the Grand' Place; 24-hour public transport tickets, hotel reservations, and car hire. Open Mon.-Sat. 9am-6pm; Sun. 9am-6pm (summer), 10am-2pm (winter). Closed December-February.

The **Office of Tourism** can help organize group or individual stays in Brussels for special

Sitting in a tranquil beer-café – a favorite pastime

rates, provide multilingual hostesses for fairs, exhibitions and congresses, and provide information about all kinds of cultural, sports and tourist events both within and outside the city. The information center on the Rue Marché-aux-Herbes 63 is open every day, all year. From June to September, it is open 9am-7pm; the rest of the year Mon.-Sat. 9am-6pm, Sun. 1-5pm (winter), 9am-6pm (spring). Vacation periods and long weekends, 9am-7pm. Closed Sat. and Sun. between 1-2pm. Closed January 1 and December 25.

Tourist information booths have also been set up in the North and South Railway Stations, and in the luggage hall of the airport. (Tel. 722.30.00/01).

The Chambers of Commerce can be found in the Telephone book under "Chambres de Commerce". Embassies are listed under "Ambassades". The Foreign Affairs office is at Rue des Quatre Bras 2 (Tel. 238.25.11).

Keeping in Touch

Radio and TV programs are in Flemish and French. On the Flemish TV channels, movies and interviews are shown in the original language. BBC can be picked up, and English-language newspapers are available on many newsstands; they include the *International Herald Tribune*, the *Wall Street Journal*, *USA Today*, *The London Times*, *The Financial Times* and other major journals. Many magazines in English can also be found. The *Bulletin* is an English-language weekly published locally, containing articles and entertainment listings.

PHONES

The Telephone prefix for Brussels is 02. Public Telephones take 5-franc coins. Booths from which international calls can be made and Telegrams sent are marked with a series of flags from different countries. The phone book has an English index.

Telephone calls from hotels can be subject to expensive surcharges. Before placing a long-distance call from your hotel, ask how much it will cost. Some hotels have made agreements to limit surcharges, but you may find it worth your while to use one of the Belgacom telephone offices for making long-distance calls. These offices have a number of booths: you will be assigned one where you can place your call and pay after you have finished.

Belgacom telephone offices:
Blvd. de l'Impératrice 17: Open daily 8am-10pm. Tel. 513.89.81.
Airport: Open daily 7am-10pm. Tel. 720.24.15.

Some telephones accept Telecard. International direct dial is also available.

Telegrams may be sent by phone. Dial 1325, by fax 1335 for general service. They can also be sent from Belgacom offices (above), also your hotel may be able to send one for you.

POST-OFFICES

Post offices are usually open 9am-5pm weekdays. The office at Ave. Fonsny 48A (Gare du Midi) is open around the clock every day, including weekends and holidays. Currency exchanges can be made from 9am-5pm only. Tel. 217.03.51.

Other post offices are at Centre Monnaie, the Gare Centrale, the Gare du Nord, Rue du Progrés 80, Bourse, Palais de Justice and Blvd. Charlemagne 1.

ENGLISH LANGUAGE BOOK STORES

English-language book stores, include *House of Paperbacks*: Chaussee de Waterloo 813 (Tel. 343.11.22); *W.H. Smith & Son*: Blvd. Adolphe Max 71 (Tel. 219.27.08); *Strathmore*

Bookshop: Rue St-Lambert 110 (Tel. 771.92.00); *Libris*: Ave. de la Toison d'Or 29 (Tel. 511.64.00).

Business Hours

Office hours are usually 8:30am-noon and 1-5pm. Appointments are required, and it is polite to shake hands both when arriving and leaving.

Shops are open Mon-Sat. 10am-6pm or 7pm. Small shops may close for lunch and stay open later. Department Stores may stay open until 8 or 9pm on Friday. The stores are open regular hours on Saturday. Some shops catering to tourists, and those selling food or flowers are open on Sunday.

Banking hours are Mon-Fri. 9:15am-3:30pm; most banks close for an hour or two for lunch. Foreign exchange offices at the North and South Railway Stations are open daily 7am-11pm and in the Gare Centrale 8am-9pm weekdays, and 9am-5pm Sunday. These banks operate at the airport: B.B.L is open 7am-9:45pm, Kredietbank is open 7:15am-9:45pm. Société Générale de Banque is open 7am-9:45pm.

Tipping

The custom in Brussels is to tip on almost every occasion. Here are a few guidelines.

In movies and theaters, 20 francs per person to the usher or usherette.

In restaurants, a service charge of 16.5% is included, but round up the amount a few francs for very good service.

In cloakrooms, 50 to 100 francs.

The Grand' Place, Brussels' central square

In hotels, service is included, but give a personal tip to the chambermaid and porter for good service.

Hairdressers may include service. If not, leave 20% at the cash desk.

In taxis, service is included, but the fare can be rounded up.

In public toilets, 10 to 15 francs unless a service charge is posted.

Luggage porters, about 60 francs per item.

Medical Services

Most doctors in Brussels speak English, and so do many of the hospital and emergency personnel. Standby medical service is available at all times in the city. Dial 479.18.18, or 648.80.00 for information.

An emergency dental service operates evenings and weekends. It is available on weekdays 9pm-7am and on weekends from 7am Saturday to 7am Monday. On holidays, it is also available 7am-9pm. Tel. 426.10.26 or 428.58.88.

Pharmacies take turns being on-call at night and on weekends. The name of a pharmacist on-duty in a particular area will be posted in all the local pharmacy windows. Hotels can also assist guests in locating pharmacies on-duty.

Fairs, Conventions

A huge complex of exhibition halls has been built at Heysel in the northern part of the city near the Atomium to accommodate medium to large sized fairs. In addition, the city has a number of facilities for shows and exhibitions, including the Rogier Center near the North Railway Station.

Information is available from the Brussels Congress Department of the Tourist Office (Tel. 504.02.75, fax 513.07.50. Brussels hostesses are available to help with shows, trade fairs, exhibitions and congresses.

The Union of International

Associations, Rue Washington 38-40, Ixelles (Tel. 640.41.09, fax 646.05.25) is open weekdays 9am-5pm. It is a meeting place and work center for many non-governmental, non-profit organizations. Brussels claims to be the most important center after Paris for such groups, ranking ahead of London and Geneva.

The International Press Center is at Blvd. Charlemagne 1. Tel. 238.08.11. Brussels also claims to be the most important press center after Washington, D.C., with 350 journalists in residence.

BRUSSELS – AREA BY AREA

The Shape of the City

A glance at the map of Brussels will immediately reveal large green and blue patches, which represent the many parks and lakes in the city. There are fewer of these as you get closer to the center of the city, which is more or less pentagonal in shape, defined by the boulevards which surround it. These boulevards were built in the 19th century in place of the walls which once surrounded the Old City.

Our routes will be concentrated in this part of town, and will begin in the center of this area, in the narrow little streets which form the heart of the Old City. In the middle of this area is the Grand' Place, which is the starting point of our routes, and the main tourist site in Brussels.

Within this more or less pentagonal area, the southeastern part is higher, and is called the upper city. Here you will find, among other sites, Musées Royaux des Beaux-Arts, Place Royale, Palais de Justice, Parliament and Parc de Bruxelles, which is the main park in this area. In the lower city is the Grand' Place, the famous Manneken-Pis – the symbol of Brussels – and some of Brussels' main shopping centers. The slope between the upper and lower parts of the city also has its share of interesting sites, and here you will find the Cathedral of St. Michel, Place du Sablon and Mont des Arts.

From the central pentagon the main roads of Brussels lead out in different directions. Avenue Louise, in which you will find many prestigious shops, leads to Bois de la Cambre, the biggest park in Brussels; Rue de Loi leads to the EEC Building and Parc du Cinquantenaire; Rue Royale leads to Laeken, the Atomium and the royal estate; Boulevard Leopold II leads to the Basilique church; and Chaussée de Monts leads to Anderlecht.

An *autostrada* surrounds Brussels in an enormous ring road, which has interchanges with major roads leading to Antwerp, Ghent, Bruges, Ostende, Cologne, Luxembourg and Paris.

The Brewery Museum in the Grand' Place

Grand' Place – The Crowning Jewel

Metro: Gare Centrale, Bourse
Tram: 52, 55, 58
Bus: 29, 60, 63, 65, 71

In Brussels, all roads lead to the Grand' Place. The heart of the city can easily be covered on foot and this is the best way of seeing it.

Grand' Place, the central square in Brussels, is a place of amazing beauty and undoubtedly one of the most beautiful squares in Europe. Victor Hugo claimed that it was indeed the most beautiful square in Europe.

Until the 12th century this area was covered in swamps and once the swamps were drained the square became the market of Brussels. In succeeding years the square reflected the changes and developments that shaped the character and destiny of the city of Brussels.

The central location of the square has meant that over the years wealthy citizens have built their homes and established their businesses in this vicinity.

The 17th century ushered in the greatest

The Hôtel de Ville towers magestically over the Grand' Place

Grand' Place – considered to be one of the most beautiful squares in Europe

period of prosperity. The guilds had became a powerful force, and they began buying areas around the square and competing against one another to build the most beautiful and impressive buildings. The beautiful Hôtel de Ville (City Hall) set the tone concerning the beauty and character of the buildings, but the styles were different.

At the end of the 17th century the development process was halted for many years when the armies of Louis XIV, King of France advanced on Brussels, and bombarded it, especially the square in the middle of the city. The Hotel de Ville was almost all that remained of the glory of the square.

The citizens of Brussels lost no time in rebuilding the square, and within 4 years the buildings were completed. Many buildings were completely rebuilt while others were substantially restored. Gilt exteriors and marble and bronze statues were added to the walls and roofs of the buildings. The results, which we see today, create an architectural harmony which is rich and breathtaking.

A rich variety of shapes and colors at the flower market

The marketing center of Brussels is no longer in the

THE GRAND' PLACE

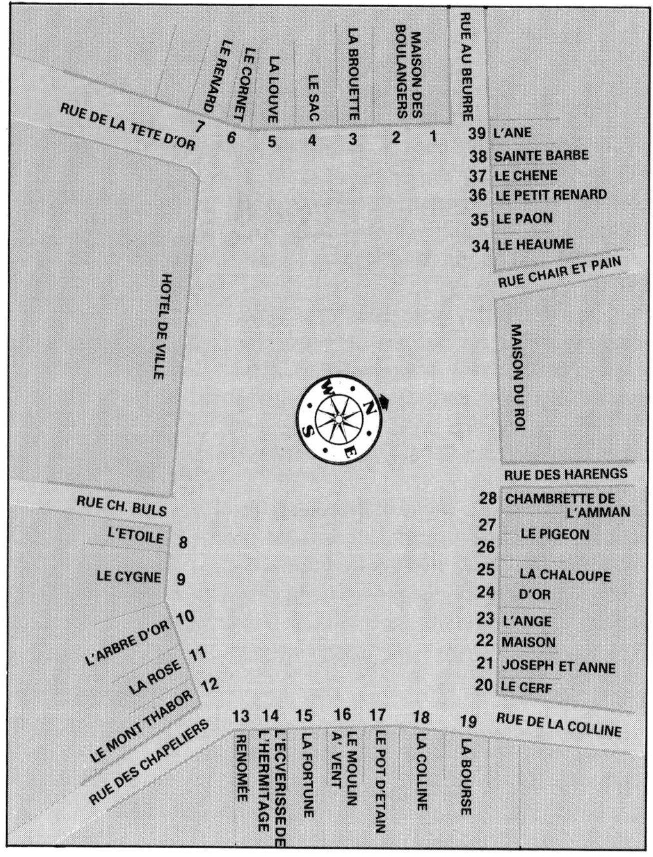

square. The last trace is the small flower market which takes place daily in the middle of the square. The square is nevertheless always bustling with people strolling along and admiring the buildings, sipping coffee in the elegant cafés or dining in the stylish restaurants.

A single visit to the square is not enough, because one cannot absorb and digest all the architectural wealth of the square at once, and also because the square has different faces at different times. If you first visit during the day, you must return at night,

Birds, popular and plentiful, at the bird market

when the buildings are illuminated with artificial light. In summer there is a sound and light show – colored lights are projected onto the Hôtel de Ville and classical music is played in the background. On Sunday mornings the square acquires a different character when the **bird market** takes place here. The Sunday morning bird market goes on all year round. Dealers and private individuals congregate with wire or wooden cages, and occasionally wine cartons, full of birds to sell. Prospective buyers stroll among them, sometimes stopping to bargain and buy.

Tiny songbirds are popular, parakeets are plentiful and one corner is devoted to domestic fowl. The most interesting bargaining goes on for the homing pigeons. Pigeon racing is possibly the most popular sport in Belgium – even more popular than football.

There are two main events in the Grand' Place which you should not miss. The most well known is the **Ommegang**, which takes place on the first Tuesday and first Thursday of July. This is an aristocratic historic event which originated in the year 1549, when the leaders of the city organised a celebration for the King Charles V who ruled the Lowland countries as well as Spain and parts of Italy.

The second major event in the square is the **flower show** which takes place every two years in the summer when the square is covered in a carpet of blossoms laid out in a huge geometric design. A show is held in mid-August every two years, in the years ending with even numbers, i.e. 1994, 1996, 1998, etc. These two events have influenced the summer festivals in many other cities in Belgium and today almost every city has its Ommegang and its flower show. Besides these events, there are many others on summer evenings and you can get details from a branch of the tourist information office. The problem, however, with such events, is that the stages which are set up obscure the magnificent architecture of the buildings. You will, therefore, have to return to the square at some other time.

Before beginning a tour of the square, take into consideration the fact that a visit takes some time because each building has its own distinct character, either architectural or historical.

The Hôtel de Ville with its high tower

Standing out against the Italo-Brabant baroque buildings is a splendid Gothic masterpiece, the **Hôtel de Ville** (The Town Hall). The Hôtel de Ville can be visited only on regular guided tours. (Open 9:30am-12:15pm and 1:45-4pm. Sun. and during holidays 10am-noon and 2-4pm. The guided tours are cancelled when sessions of the City Council or receptions are held).

The Hôtel de Ville is lopsided because of additions to the original (not through a mistake, which according to popular legend impelled the builder to throw himself off the tower in despair). The right side is not as long as the left and the porch is not in the center of the tower, because of instructions given to the architect that he must not encroach upon the Rue de la Tête d'Or. The Hôtel de Ville was built in 1402 by Jacques van Tienen and additions were made in 1444, when Charles the Bold, aged nine, laid the foundation stone for the new wing. The narrow fretwork tower, the work of Jan van Ruysbroeck, was added at that time; it is 300 feet high and the weather-vane (a depiction of St. Michael, the city's patron, defeating a demon) adds another 15 feet. A second addition was made to the back of the building in the 1700's.

The 137 sculptures placed on the exterior walls of the building were carved and placed there in the 19th century as replacements for older sculptures, some of which can be seen at the adjacent Maison du Roi. The sculpture on the front façade represents the rulers of Brabant until the end of the 16th century. The sculptures on the side walls represent people who have used their talents to glorify the city of Brussels.

A number of houses were in the way of the alteration and had to be torn down, but at least one of them, De Moor, is commemorated on a capital of a pillar. Look for a sleeping Moor and his harem. Other capitals depict "the drinking monks" and a particular punishment called "Strappado", in which a criminal was strapped into a chair and dumped into a pond.

We will go in through the main entrance. On our right is an entrance which leads to a staircase to the upper balcony of the tower

The broad and elegant Grand' Place is full of activity at all times of the day

(open only on Sundays) from which you can gaze out at a beautiful view of the city center.

The main entrance leads to an interior courtyard in which there are two fountains decorated with sculptures of bearded figures which symbolize the rivers Meuse and Scheldt, the two biggest rivers in Belgium.

A guided tour of the building passes through the rooms which are still used today by the mayor and the city council. The rooms were furnished in different periods and in different styles, but all of them reflect great wealth. Antique tapestries from 1618, which decorate some of the rooms are one of the main attractions of a visit to the building. The Van Moer Room is one of the most interesting in the building, not so much for the style, as for the pictures on the wall. The room is named after the artist who painted scenes of Brussels in the 19th century when the Senne river still flowed between the buildings of the city.

A figure representing justice at Le Renard (the fox), guild house of the haberdashers

From the Hôtel de Ville, cross the Rue de la Tête d'Or (Golden Head). On the right, facing the Town Hall is **Le Renard** (the Fox), guild house of the haberdashers, topped by a statue of their patron St. Nicholas. The reliefs on the ground floor, like the façade of the building itself, were done in the Italo-Flemish style, which was widespread in the middle of the 17th century. These reliefs represent the different handicrafts with which the merchants of this guild were involved. Above the balcony of the first floor are five statues made by Marc de Vos and Jan van Delen. The central figure is blindfolded and holds a pair of scales in one hand and a sword in the other. The figure represents the

allegory of Justice. The four figures flanking the central figure represent the four parts of the world which were known at the time – Africa, Europe, Asia and America – from which the merchants brought their goods.

Next is **Le Cornet** (the Horn), house of the boatmen. It's no surprise that its gable is in the shape of a ship's stern from the 17th century. Two golden lions recline on the roof of the building, on either side of the Spanish royal coat of arms. Below them are four figures which represent the sea winds. These figures surround the relief of Charles II, the king of Spain who also ruled the Lowlands in the 17th century.

La Louve (the She-Wolf) belonged to the archers' guild; its name comes from the Romulus and Remus relief above the door. This building is slightly older than the others in the square because it was hardly damaged by the French bombardment which took place in 1695. The building was built in 1691. The figures on either side of the 2nd floor are allegories of Truth, Falsehood, Peace and Discord. On the top part of the building, in the pediment above four medallions bearing the images of Roman emperors, is a relief of Apollo shooting an arrow at a snake.

Le Sac (the Sack) was the guild house of the cabinet-makers and coopers, and two levels which survived the bombardment are from the first half of the 16th century. The façade of the next house was also saved – **La Brouette** (the Wheelbarrow), house of the tanners. A statue of their patron, St. Gilles, stands in a niche at the top.

Apollo, shooting an arrow at a snake – atop the building once belonging to the archers' guild

One of the grandest houses is at the corner of the Rue au Beurre, La **Maison des Boulangers** or Roi d'Espagne. It was the bakers' house. The bust of Bishop Saint Aubert, the patron, looks over the doorway and the bust of Charles II, King of Spain, adorns the third floor. The upper part of the building is built in the Italian style, unlike the other buildings which are built in Renaissance style typical of the Lowlands. On the balustrade of the roof are six statues which represent Force, Wheat, Wind, Fire, Water and Foresight.

The first two floors of the building are used today as a café/bar. A stuffed horse which stands in the middle of the ground floor enhances the country ambience of the bar. On a hot day it is refreshing to sit at one of the outdoor tables and enjoy one of the 700 different beers sold in Brussels. The waiters today still wear the same type of apron which we see in Pieter Breughel's famous painting, *The Village Wedding*.

The next group of houses are not so elaborate. In order, they are **L'Ane** (the Donkey) and **La Ronce Couronnée** (the Crowned Curl) or Sainte Barbe. They were restored at the beginning of the 20th century. **Le Chene** (the Oak Tree) and **Le Petit Renard** (the Little

Fox) were built under the same roof and adorned by dormer windows. Then come **Le Paon** (the Peacock) and **Le Héaume** (the Helmet).

Cross the Rue Chair et Pain and stop in front of the **Maison du Roi** (King's House). Despite its name no king ever lived in this building. It started as a store used by the bakers; the Meat Hall just behind it was its twin. It was converted into a jail, then into a tax office, when it was named first the Duke's House, and then the King's House once the duke was crowned. When the French conquered Belgium, they changed the name to Public House. It served as the court house and war-council building, and regressed into such poor condition that it had to be torn down. It was rebuilt between 1873 and 1895 and now houses the **Musée de la Ville de Bruxelles** (Museum of the City of Brussels). Tel. 511.27.42. Admission fee. Open Mon.-Fri. 10am-12:30pm, 1:30-5pm, Oct.-March till 4pm. Public holidays 10am-1pm. Guided tours on request, by T.I.B., Tel. 513.89.40.

The ornate façade of the Musée de la Ville de Bruxelles

The museum displays the urban and geographic history of the city, and the ground floor is devoted to art. On the immediate right of the entrance you can see *The Marriage Procession* by Pieter Breughel, as well as altar pieces from the beginning of the 16th century, a number of tapestries from this period and an exhibit which represents the development of sculpture in Brussels in the last few centuries.

On the first floor there is an interesting

exhibit of faience porcelain and other ceramics and silverware, which reflect the cultural and economic golden age of Brussels during the 14th and 15th centuries. The top floor is devoted to an entertaining exhibit of Manneken-Pis clothing. The exhibit contains some 400 costumes which have been sent to the famous statue since the 18th century. The exhibit in fact constitutes a collection of national costumes from all over the world.

At the Musée de la Ville de Bruxelles

Don't miss the allegorical decorations and the statuette of the chicken on a spit – the *Bruxellois* have the nickname *kiekenfretters*, "chicken eaters".

Across the Petite Rue des Harengs (Small Street of Herrings), is yet another group of houses. La Chambrette de l'Amman (the Amman's Little Room) and Le Pigeon stand at Numbers 27 and 28. **Le Pigeon** was the painters' house, but the guild was so poor that it had to sell the land to an architect after the bombardment. The architect designed a reconstruction in a classic style. Notice the Venetian window on the first floor, which gives an original stamp to the building. La **Chambrette de l'Amman** used to be called the Guild of the Goldsellers. Today it is known by the name Aux Armes de Brabant because on the façade of the building there is a symbol of the province. Victor Hugo lived here in 1852, when he fled France, he wrote about the city in *Les Miserables*.

La Chaloupe d'Or at Numbers 24-25 was built in the Italo-Flemish style and belonged to the tailors' guild. St. Boniface gives his

blessing from the roof. **L'Ange** (the Angel) at Number 23 is in the florid Italo-Flemish style, unlike **Le Cerf** (the Stag) at Number 20 and **Joseph et Anne** next door which are simple bourgeois houses.

The **Dukes of Brabant House** looks like a rich palace stretching across one end of the Grand' Place. It is actually seven different houses: La Bourse (the Exchange), La Colline (the Hill), Le Pot d'Etain (the Pewter Tankard), Le Moulin a Vent (the Windmill), La Fortune (the Fortune) and L'Ecverisse de

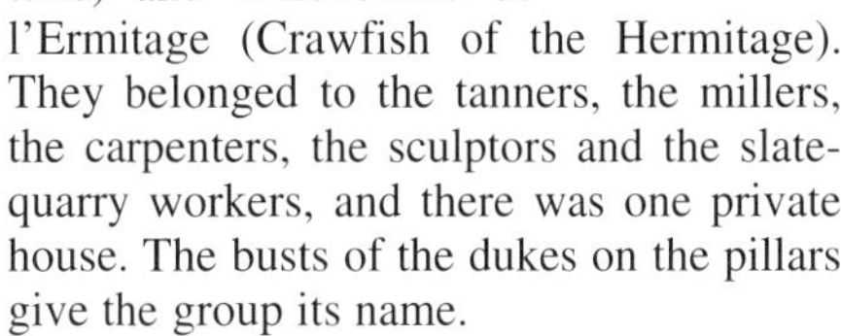
l'Ermitage (Crawfish of the Hermitage). They belonged to the tanners, the millers, the carpenters, the sculptors and the slate-quarry workers, and there was one private house. The busts of the dukes on the pillars give the group its name.

The next tiny street, Rue des Chapeliers, is the place where a fight broke out between

Displays of the different beer making processes at the Brewery Museum

La Maison du Cygne – once the butchers' guild house

two great French poets, Verlaine and Rimbaud. Verlaine was a better writer than he was a shot, but he was imprisoned for six months for "wounds inflicted" on Rimbaud.

Le Mont Thabor and **La Rose** are good examples of middle-class houses of the late 17th and early 18th centuries. **L'Arbre d'Or** (Golden Tree) is now called the Brewers' House. Its façade is adorned with a beer barrel decorated with barley and hops, and sure enough, it houses the city's **Brewery Museum**. You can sip a beer here, and admire the collection of draught handles and the replica of an 18th century brewery. (Grand' Place 10. Tel. 511.49.87. Admission fee. Open Mon.-Fri. 10am-noon and 2-5pm. Also open Saturday mornings between April and October.

Le Cygne (Swan) started out as a tavern, but soon became the butchers' guild house. The Belgian Workmen's Union was established here in 1885.

Last comes one of the oldest houses on the Grand' Place, **L'Étoile** (Star). It actually has been rebuilt on an archway over the sidewalk, having been torn down in 1852 to improve traffic flow. The first reference to the building dates back to the 13th century when it was the office of the Amman, whose duty it was to oversee beheadings from its balcony. The building, which was rebuilt at the end of the last century was one of the last structures to be rebuilt in the square. The big bronze plate on the side of the house is dedicated to Everard't Serclaes, Brussels' first hero, who delivered the city from the troops of the Count of Flanders in the 14th century. He was assassinated, and died in this house. On the engraved plaque, his arm and the nose of the dog at his feet are shiny, because over the years people have been rubbing them for luck. If you need to relax and take a break at this point, there are many cafés on the square, offering coffee or a beer.

Around the Grand' Place

Metro: Gare Centrale, Bourse
Tram: 52, 55, 58, 62
Bus: 29, 34, 48, 63, 71

The streets around the Grand' Place are named for various food markets that once took place here – bread, butter, cheese and meat. The markets are gone, but good food is still close to the hearts of the Bruxellois and a number of excellent eateries are concentrated in this area. Cross the Rue Marche aux Herbes and step into the **Ilot Sacré**. Restaurants line the sides of the narrow walkway Petite Rue de Bouchers and its surroundings, and they are always busy. Tempting arrays of fish are iced down out front, and you can stand and watch the experts shucking oysters or arranging "plateaux" of seafood.

Down a very narrow alley is **Toone** (follow the signs), a beer tavern that is the only survivor of the popular marionette theaters of Brussels. It is at Impasse Schuddeveld, reached from Petite Rue des Bouchers. (Tel. 511.71.37. Admission fee. Open during intermission of marionette performances.).

A lively café at the Galeries Saint Hubert

Toone is short for Antione, a local family, who has run the theater for many years. The building dates from 1696, having been rebuilt in what was then the butchers' quarter immediately after the bombardment by the French.

The theater was founded in 1830, and soon became known for the quality of its productions particularly the stage sets, costumes and the subtlety of interpretation. One of its puppet-characters is *Woltje*, comparable to Lyon's *Guignol* or London's *Punch*, and equally dear to the people of Brussels.

The streets in the vicinity of Ilot Sacré acquire a special

character on summer evenings when street artists perform here, and dozens of artists and craftsmen come here to show and sell their work and to draw portraits of the passers by. On these evenings the square reminds one of Montmartre in Paris.

At the Toone, a theater specializing in marionette performances

If you wander through the Ilot Sacré, you will undoubtedly stumble upon the **Galeries Saint Hubert** which stretch from the Rue Marché aux Herbes to Rue d'Arenberg, crossing Rue des Bouchers. Built in 1846, they are the first galleries in Europe containing shops, restaurants and theaters. If you turn right at the end (Rue d'Arenberg) you will reach the Cathedral and the Central Station (see "Art and Royalty – from Mont des Art to the Cathedral"). We will, however, turn left here, and continue as far as De Brouckére, where you will find **Théâtre Royal de la Monnaie** (the Opera House). Tel. 218.12.11. Open Mon.-Sat. 11am-6pm. It takes its name from the Hotel des Monnaies which was in front of it. It was here, in 1830, that the revolt against William I, King of the United Kingdom of the Netherlands, broke out when the audience burst out of the theater, and hoisted the

The entry to the Galeries Saint Hubert

tricolor flag of Brabant above the Hotel de Ville.

The existing neoclassical appearance of the building with its triangular crown and carving representing the harmony of human passions dates back to 1855 when the building was rebuilt after a fire destroyed the original building.

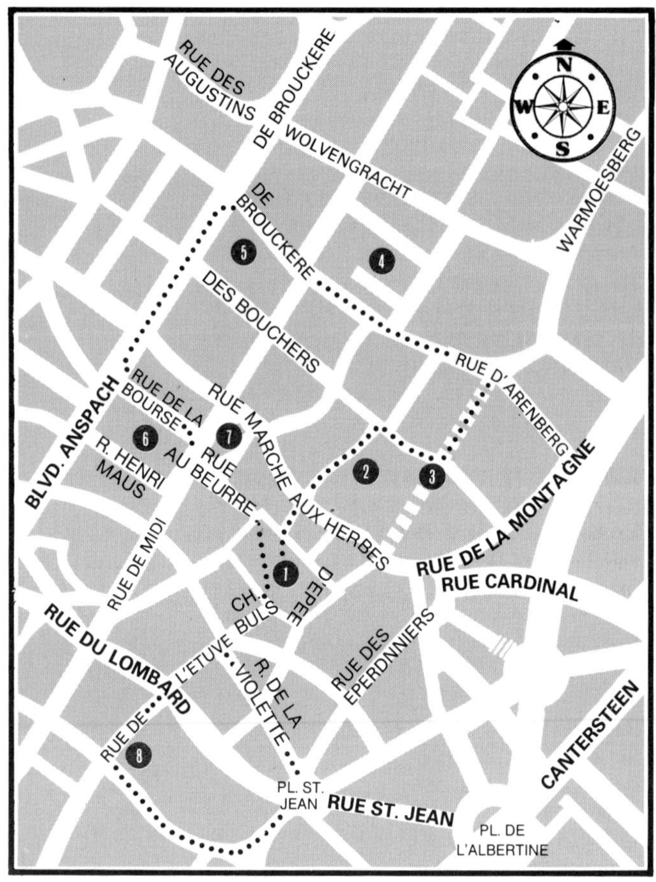

AROUND THE GRAND' PLACE

1. Grand' Place
2. Ilot Sacre
3. Galeries Saint Hubert
4. Théatre Royal de la Monnaie
5. Anspach Shopping Center
6. Bourse
7. Saint Nicolas Church
8. Manneken-Pis

The neoclassical façade of the Théâtre Royal de la Monnaie

Nearby is the **Anspach Shopping Center**, which contains a **Wax Museum** (Blvd. Anspach 36. Tel. 217.60.23. Tram 52, 55, 58, or 91. Admission fee. Open daily 10am-6pm). An English-language leaflet sold at the desk explains the historic tableaux. A 100 well-known characters in magnificent costumes recreate the history of Belgium in 18 steps.

Walk along the Boulevard Anspach, a large shopping street, toward the **Bourse** (Stock Exchange), on Rue Henri Maus 2, which was built in 1873 by architect Leon Suys (neoclassical style). It can be visited weekdays on request. Tel. 509.12.11, entry free.

Turn onto Rue de la Bourse, and go as far as **Saint Nicolas Church**, which dates back to the origins of Brussels, but of course has undergone rebuilding and restoration. It contains a painting by Peter Paul Rubens, *The Virgin and the Sleeping Child*, and a number of beautiful altars. The medallions on the stalls tell the story of Saint Nicolas.

In its early days, a little stream ran around inside the church. (Tel. 267.51.64)

Return to the Grand' Place along the Rue au Beurre, stopping at the venerable **Bakery Dandoy** for a look around and a taste of the Brussels specialty *pain à la Grecque*.

Manneken-Pis – the symbol of the city, representing its good humor and individual spirit

Now walk in another direction from the Grand' Place, down Chaussee Buls, which becomes Rue de l'Etuve, to look at the **Manneken-Pis**, a naughty little boy who represents the free spirit of Brussels. He is a symbol of the city just as the Statue of Liberty is a symbol of New York, and the Eiffel Tower is a symbol of Paris. There are many variations of the Manneken-Pis legend, but he certainly represents the spirit of individual freedom and good humor of the people of Brussels.

The first Manneken-Pis is believed to have been a 14th-century stone fountain. One story says he was the son of a local ruler. He was caught by a witch as he was relieving himself on her front door, and she was so angry that she changed him to stone!

In 1619, he was cast in bronze by Jerome Duquesnoy. That statue was destroyed and another cast in 1630, but that did not survive either. "Little Julian", as he is sometimes called, was kidnapped for the first time by the English in 1745, and two years later was stolen by the French. Again in 1817, a Frenchman kidnapped him and he was found broken into pieces. The fragments were used to make the mould from which the present statue was cast.

The Manneken-Pis has captured the hearts

of people the world over, and hardly any tourist fails to get a glimpse of him. Many send him gifts of costumes, a tradition begun in 1698 by the Elector of Bavaria. Louis XV of France sent him one, too. Some of his wardrobe is displayed in the Musée Ville de Bruxelles (see "Grand' Place – The Crowning Jewel") and all the suits are brought out for special exhibitions.

Manneken-Pis, dressed in one of its many costumes

In high season, his clothes are changed on alternate days: he has his own valet. For special celebrations, he is dressed appropriately. On the anniversary of the liberation of Brussels, he wears the uniform of the Belgian Army Corps which first entered the city. On November 21, St. Verhaeghen's Day, he is dressed in the costume of a student in honor of the founder of the university.

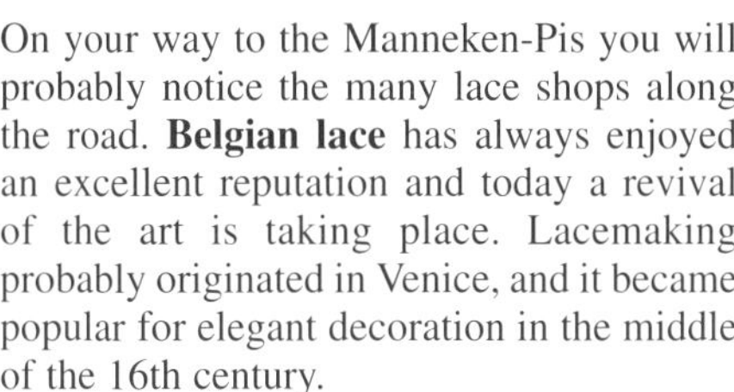

On your way to the Manneken-Pis you will probably notice the many lace shops along the road. **Belgian lace** has always enjoyed an excellent reputation and today a revival of the art is taking place. Lacemaking probably originated in Venice, and it became popular for elegant decoration in the middle of the 16th century.

When Colbert founded the *Manufactures royales du point de France* in Paris during the reign of Louis XIV, he brought 30 lace-makers there from Venice, and 200 from Flanders.

The famous Belgian lace incorporating delicately woven designs

Different towns in the Low Countries developed individual styles, which were appropriately named: Ghent, Bruges, Lilles, Malines, Brussels, Valenciennes etc. There is a special vocabulary to describe the different types of lace, which vary according to the method of pro-

A relaxing chat at the Galeries Saint Hubert

duction (needle or bobbin), type of thread used, weave, design, motif and material.

Lace was used for religious garments and veils, but its main use as elegant adornment reached a peak in the 18th century, when Brussels had 10,000 lacemakers.

Lacemaking suffered in the French Revolution, and was dealt a fatal blow by the invention of a machine which could make net 6000 times faster than it could be made by hand.

A statuette outside the Bourse building

Nevertheless, the secrets of the handiwork have survived, and today schools and clubs are teaching increasing numbers of students how to make lace. Among them are the Kantcentrum (Lace Center) at Bruges, the Workshop of Contemporary Lace run by the city of Brussels and professional courses sponsored by the town of Binche. A Lace Workshop is run by the Royal Museums of Art and History in Brussels. Information is available from the tourist office.

Lacemaking is, above all, a

creative art, and the new generation of lace-makers is not content to merely copy the lace of the past, no matter how exquisite. Modern and contemporary laces are being created in the Belgian schools and lace centers.

At Rue de la Violette, you may wish to visit the **Costume and Lace Museum** (Musée des Costumes et Dentelle) at Number 6. It houses a collection of chasubles and ecclesiastical habits and a 19th century passementerie workshop. (Tel. 512.77.09. Admission fee. Open Mon.-Fri. 10am-12:30pm and 1:30-5pm. October-March till 4pm. Weekends and holidays 2-4:30pm.)

Either the Rue de la Violette or Rue du Chêne (beside Manneken-Pis) will take you to Place St. Jean, and from there Rue St. Jean leads to Place d'Albertine and the Mont des Arts.

The Bourse – Brussels' Stock Exchange

Antiques and Flea Markets – Sablon to Place du Jeu de Balle

Metro: Porte Namur
Tram: 92, 93, 94
Bus: 20, 34, 71, 95, 96

The best day to do this tour is Saturday if you want to explore the flea markets. We begin our tour at the Petit Sablon, which is approximately halfway between Place Royale and Palais de Justice.

The lush green of the Petit Sablon

The **Petit Sablon** is a garden enclosed by a superb balustrade of hand-wrought iron. Forty-eight bronze statues, representing the guilds of Brussels, stand atop little Gothic columns along the balustrade. In the center of the garden is a statue of the Counts of Egmont and Hornes, who were beheaded in 1568 for their struggles against Spanish rule. Ten other statues around the inside of the garden represent humanists of the 16th century.

The Musée Instrumental (Musical Instruments Museum) in the **Conservatoire de Musique** has some 6000 exhibits, and the oldest items date from the Bronze Age. (Petit Sablon 17. Tel. 511.35.95. Entry free. Open Tues.-Sat. 2:30-4:30pm; Sun.

10:30am-12:30pm. Closed Mon. and public holidays. The adjacent synagogue dates from 1878.

On the other side of Rue de la Régence at No. 36 is the **Church of Notre-Dame des Victoires du Sablon**. (Tel. 426.87.68. Open April-October 3-5pm) The original chapel was built by the Guild of Crossbowmen in 1304. It was expanded in the 15th and 16th centuries, and became a lavishly decorated Gothic church.

Near the church to the northwest is the **Place du Grand Sablon**. Today the square is a center for antique dealers. The buildings around the square are old craftsmen's houses which give the square a certain charm. The ground floors serve mostly as shops of antique dealers (quite expensive) or as coffee shops or confectionery shops. Don't leave Brussels without sampling the Belgian chocolate, try the famous *Godiva* chocolates.

On weekends there is a lot of commercial activity in this square. Near the church, tents are put up, and in the winter gas heaters are lit. In the tents the antique dealers offer their wares, you can find old books and old photographs from all over the world, primitive African art, old paintings and other antiques. If you get hungry there is always a woman selling mussels at the edge of the market. She scoops the mussels out of boiling water, separates them from their shells and gives them to you inside a little plastic box.

Place du Grand Sablon

On the northern edge of the square on the other side of Bodenbroek street and near the church, you will find a shop which specializes in white household utensils. If you feel like some refreshment there are some coffee shops and restaurants around the square, or you could go inside the small arcade of shops in the middle of the southern edge of the square. Here, among the stylish antique shops you will find a pleasant restaurant on a patio in the center of the arcade.

The Fountain of Minerva, in the center of the square, was given to the city of Brussels in 1715 as a thanksgiving gift from Lord Thomas Bruce, the Earl of Ailesbury and friend of James II. The Scottish aristocrat

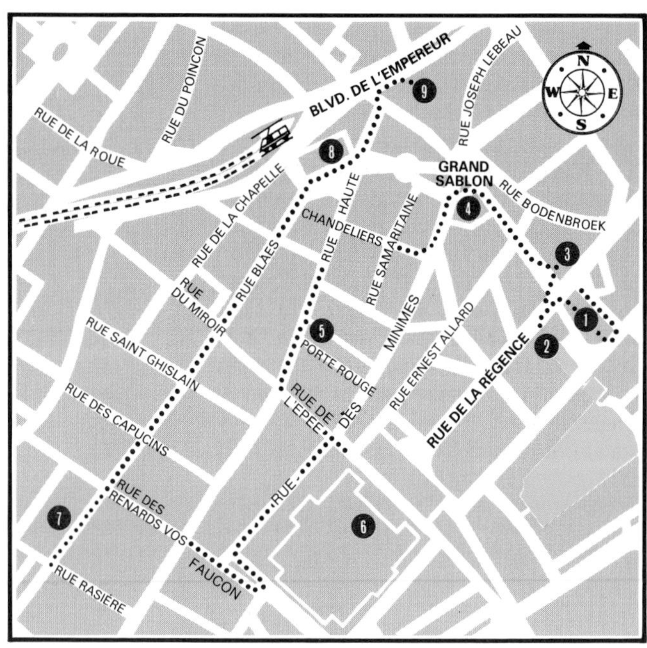

FROM SABLON TO PLACE DU JEU DE BALLE

1. Petit Sablon
2. Musée Instrumental
3. Church of Notre-Dame des Victoires du Sablon
4. The Musée Postes et Télécommunications
5. Brueghel's House
6. Palais de Justice
7. Place du Jeu de Balle
8. Church of Notre-Dame de la Chapelle
9. Tour d'Angle

The Fountain of Minerva, a gift from Lord Thomas Bruce, the Earl of Ailesbury, to the city of Brussels

was partner in the Jacobite revolt in Scotland and spent his exile in Brussels between 1696 and 1741.

The Musée Postes et Télécommunications (Post and Telecommunications Museum) is at Place du Grand Sablon 40. Tel. 511.60.60. Entry free. Open Tues.-Sat. 10am-4pm, Sun. and public holidays 10am-12:30pm. Philatelists will love this museum, which has a collection of Belgian stamps, a history of the postal service in Belgium and Zaire and a collection of communications equipment. There is also a postal train wagon at the station Bruxelles-Petite-Ile, Ave. Fonsy 48a. It is opened on request. Tel. 511.77.40.

From the Grand Sablon, turn left into Minimenstraat and then right into the narrow Chandeliers alley. Turn left again at Rue Haute. This was the neighborhood of Brueghel, whose house still stands at Rue Haute 132, at the corner of Rue de la Porte Rouge. The house is unfortunately not open to visitors. Turn left again at Rue de l'Epée; from here there is an impressive view of the Palais de Justice.

The **Palais de Justice** (Law Courts) is an immense building, built in a whole series of styles based on the Greco-Roman style.

A cosy café on the Place du Grand Sablon

(Place Poelaert, Tel. 508.61.11. Open to visitors daily 9am-4pm. Closed public holidays. Free guided tours on request). The building, which was completed in 1883 reaches a height of 300 feet and was one of the most ambitious building projects in Europe at the time. It is one of the dominant buildings in the city skyline. The building itself is high but it is also built on high ground which overlooks wide parts of the city. The green dome is surrounded by figures which symbolise Justice, Law, Strength and Mercy.

From the open space in front of Palais de Justice you can look out over the lower part of the city over the roads which brought you here. You can also use the pair of binoculars which stands here. The view is particularly good at sunset.

The Church of Notre-Dame de la Chapelle

The monument here was built in memory of the Belgian infantry who fell in both World Wars. Across the street is a British monument which was built in appreciation of the help of the Allies in World War I.

Cut across to Rue des Renards (Vossenstraat) by way of Rue Faucon to **Place du Jeu de Balle**, where the city's best-known flea market takes place daily 7am-2pm – it's bigger on weekends, of course. Turn onto Rue de la Rasière. Off that street are half a dozen little streets named after craftsmen who once lived there: Orfevres (goldsmiths), Brodeurs (embroiderers), Chaisiers (chair makers), Tonneliers (coopers), Charpentiers (carpenters) and Ramoneurs (chimney sweeps). You get as much of the international flavor of Brussels here as at the official enclaves of NATO or the EEC, as you try to sort out the babble of tongues.

This part of the city is called **Marolles**; a typical working-class district of Brussels. Walk along Rue Blaes to the **Church of Notre-Dame de la Chapelle**, which was built in 1216 and designed in partly Romanesque and partly Gothic architecture. The large pilasters, capitals and columns between the chapels are typical Brabant. The ten statues on the columns represent the apostles.

Pieter Brueghel the Elder is buried here in the third chapel off the south aisle. The memorial was erected by his son Pieter. Another tomb of interest is that of Frans Anneessens, chief of the guilds who was beheaded in 1717 for defending the guilds against the Austrians.

Not far from the intersection of Rue Haute and Blvd. de l'Empereur, you can see the **Tour d'Angle**, a remnant of the 12th century ramparts. From here, you can also continue to the next route which begins at Place de l'Albertine.

Art and Royalty – Mont des Arts to the Cathedral

Metro: Chapelle Kapellekerk
Tram: 92, 93, 94
Bus: 20, 34, 38, 71, 95

The **Mont des Arts** is a park and cultural center, set on a hillside above the **Place de l'Albertine** where the Blvd. de l'Empereur meets Cantersteen. It was built in 1965 as a memorial to King Albert, the much loved and respected "Soldier King" who was killed in 1934.

Climb up through the park, past the **Albertine**. Its libraries contain more than a million books and 300,000 manuscripts. In addition, there is a Book Museum and a Printing Museum. The **Book Museum** (Musée du Livre). Tel. 519.53.57. Open Mon., Wed. and Sat. 2-4:45pm. Entry free, has a selection of prints displaying the development of the book from its earliest stages until today.

The Cathedral of St. Michel, Belgium's national church

The **Printing Museum** (Musée de l'Imprimerie) Tel. 519.53.56. (Open daily, 9am-5pm; closed Sun., public holidays, and the last week of August. Entry free.) traces the development of typographical, lithographical and binding techniques, mostly from the 19th century.

One of the more interesting sites here is a Gothic building from the beginning of the 16th century called **Chapelle de Nassau**. This is the only remnant of a much larger building (Hôtel de Nassau) which used to be, among other things, the residence of the Austrian governor of Belgium in the 18th century. The chapel is only open to the public when exhibitions take place.

Discussing affairs of the heart on the steps of the Place de l'Albertine

Under the arcade, over the street on the left is an animated clock whose giant face is illustrated with mobile figures. On top, an elegant figure strikes the hour with his stick. Its carillon is composed of 24 bells and two melodies are played alternately. Noon is the best time to hear the carillon.

Before going on to Place Royale we will turn left into Rue Ravenstein. At a curve in the road, on the opposite side, we can see the picturesque 15th century **Hotel Ravenstein**. This beautiful building is one of the last remains of the aristocratic houses of Brussels from the Burgundian period.

Further down the road at the corner we will see **Palais des Beaux-Arts** designed by Victor Horta, one of the pioneers of the Art Nouveau style in architecture. The building was built in 1928 as a one-story building so as not to block the view from the palace situated opposite. The building serves today as a cultural center, and contains among other things, the **Cinema Museum** (Musée du Cinéma). Open daily 5:30-10:30pm, admission fee. Near the museum is a cinema which shows silent movies, with a piano accompaniment. From here we retrace our steps up Rue Ravenstein.

As you reach the Place Royale, you face the **Church of Saint-Jacques-sur-Coudenberg**, which has an elegantly simple interior and a Roman style façade. The façade is a copy of a Roman peristyle. It became a "Temple of Law" during the French Revolution and was turned over to the Catholic Church in 1802. Tel. 511.78.36. (Open daily 2:30-6pm, Sun. 9am-noon and 2:30-5pm).

In the center of the Place there is a statue of Godefroid de Bouillon, who led the first crusade, and became the first Crusader King of Jerusalem.

To the right of the Place Royale are the **Musées Royaux des Beaux-Arts de Belgique** (the Royal Museums of Fine Arts) with two sections – Ancient and Modern. The **Ancient Art Museum**, Tel. 508.32.11. (Open 10-noon and 1-5pm. Closed Mon., entry free) and the **Modern Art Museum**

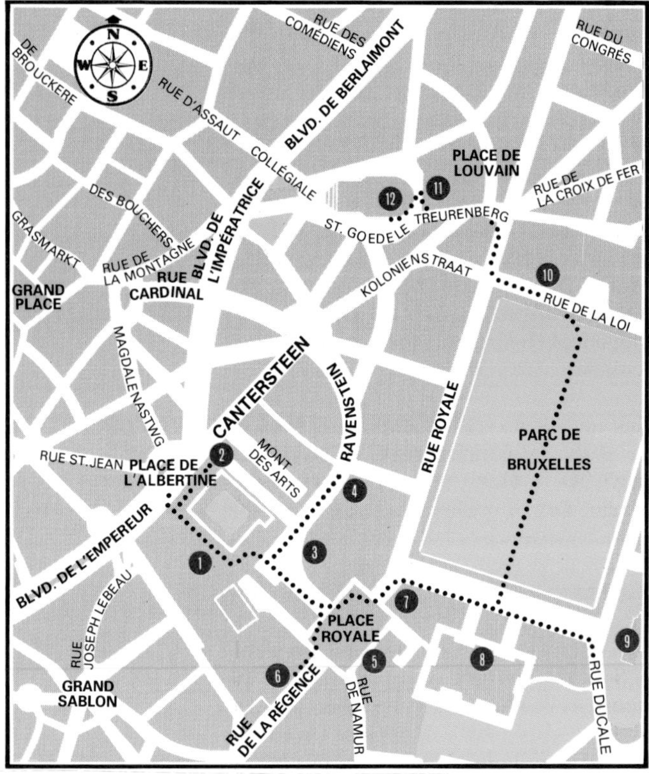

MONT DES ARTS TO THE CATHEDRAL

1. Albertine
2. Animated Clock
3. Hotel Ravenstein
4. Palais des Beaux-Arts
5. Church of St. Jacques-sur-Coudenberg
6. Musées Royaux des Beaux-Arts de Belgique
7. Hôtel Bellevue
8. Palais du Roi
9. Palais des Academies
10. Palais de la Nation
11. Pleban Tower
12. Cathedral St. Michel

(Open 10am-1pm and 2-5pm, closed Mon. and public holidays. Entry free) are both at Rue de la Regence 3. The Modern Art Museum which is underground, is entered from Place Royale 1-2 or from the Ancient Art section.

These are undoubtedly the most important museums in Brussels – especially the Ancient Art Museum, which has an outstanding collection of Flemish art.

Before going into the building, note the neo-classical façade. Built in 1885, the building has since been modernised and extended considerably. The combination of old and new architecture is reflected in the collections it houses. The four columns at the entrance support statues by De Groot of allegorical figures of the arts: Painting, Sculpture, Architecture and Music.

Pick up the museum leaflet for a nominal fee at the information desk. It looks very much like a Metro map with color-coded circuits and it makes exploration of the entire museum complex easy.

The Musées Royaux des Beaux Arts were founded by decree of Napoleon Bonaparte in 1799 and the works of art came from collections that had been confiscated during the French Revolution. The collection expanded through gifts and acquisitions over the years, and now also includes one of the best collections of 19th and 20th century art from the southern Netherlands. In 1974 the Modern Art Museum was enlarged.

Works of Flemish Primitives include *Pieta* and *The Man with the Arrow* by Van der Weyden, *Justice of Otto* by Thierry Bouts and *Christ on the Cross* by Jerome Bosch.

Among the Renaissance paintings there are many by Quentin Metsijs, Jan Motsaert, Jan Gossaert, Bernard van Orley and Pieter Aertsen, plus six outstanding paintings by Pieter Breughel, the Elder (including *Landscape with the Fall of Icarus*). The 17th century paintings include 42 works by Rubens, and many by Van Dyck, Teniers, Jan Breughel, Fyt and Snyders.

The 19th century collection covers neoclassicism, romanticism, realism, the Group of Twenty and symbolism. Wiertz, Rops, Artan, Vogels, Knopff, and Van Rysselberghe.

The 20th century collection consists mostly of Belgian works, covering expressionism, fauvism, surrealism and other contemporary trends, and here you can see works by Permeke, Rik Wouters and Magritte.

Besides the national art collection there are many works by Dutch, German, French and Italian artists – Frans Hals, Rembrandt, Cranach (the Elder), Tintoretto, Tiepolo, Lorrain, Delacroix, Seurat and Gauguin. Modern masters are well represented too, such as Francis Bacon, Max Ernst, Henry Moore and Salvador Dali, and there are also sculptures, both ancient and modern, so that the Musées Royeaux des Beaux-Arts are a real treasure for art lovers.

Hotel Ravenstein – an aristocratic house, one of the last from Brussels' Burgundian period

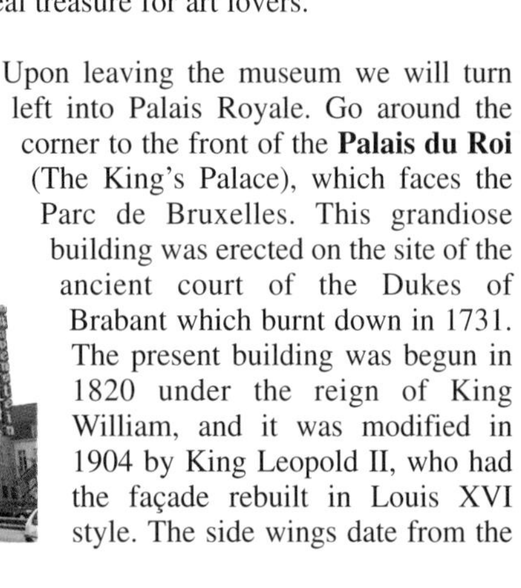

Upon leaving the museum we will turn left into Palais Royale. Go around the corner to the front of the **Palais du Roi** (The King's Palace), which faces the Parc de Bruxelles. This grandiose building was erected on the site of the ancient court of the Dukes of Brabant which burnt down in 1731. The present building was begun in 1820 under the reign of King William, and it was modified in 1904 by King Leopold II, who had the façade rebuilt in Louis XVI style. The side wings date from the

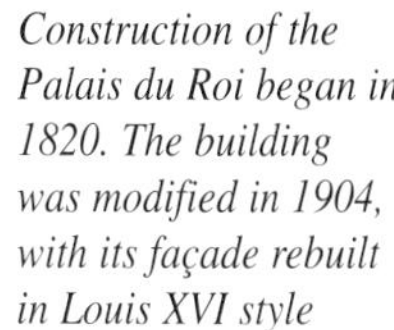

Construction of the Palais du Roi began in 1820. The building was modified in 1904, with its façade rebuilt in Louis XVI style

18th century. The bas-relief represents Belgium seated between Agriculture and Industry.

This is the official residence of Belgium's royalty and is open to the public only mid-July to August. Behind the low stone wall which surrounds the palace you will see the royal guard, which is not as colorful as the royal guard in other European courts. Changing of the Guards takes place every two hours; check with the office in charge of the guards.

The **Hôtel Bellevue** was once a residence for members of the royal family, today it houses collections of the royal family, and can be visited all year-round. It contains furniture from the 18th and 19th centuries, table settings, crystal, glazed earthenware and other objects. (Place des Palais 7. Tel. 511.44.25. Open weekdays 10am-5pm. Closed Fridays and public holidays.)

The building on our left when we are facing the Palace is **Palais des Academies**. This was built in 1823 as a residence for the Crown Prince of Orange. Today the building is used by the Belgian Royal Academy of Literature, and is closed to the public.

Not far from here at Rue Ducale, next to the right hand wing of the Palace, there is a row of buildings which serves the local aristocracy. The English poet Lord Byron lived in one of these buildings (no. 51) in 1816, and it was here that he wrote the Waterloo stanza in *Childe Harold*.

The **Parc de Bruxelles**, opposite the palace, is one of the larger pockets of green that provide escape from city stress. It was laid out in its present French form and style in 1835 and is beautifully maintained, with ornamental pools and 18th century sculptures (some are copies, the originals of which are in the Musées des Beaux-Arts for safe-keeping). In summer, there are concerts here. At the other end of the park is the **Palais de la Nation** (Belgium's Houses of Parliament), at Rue de la Loi 16. It was originally built in 1783 for the Sovereign Council of Brabant. Its majestic classical façade is surmounted by a sculpted triangle. (To visit the house, enter from Rue de Louvain 11; for the Senate – from Rue de Louvain 70. Guided tours at 10am, 11am, 2pm and 3pm. Entry free. For information on observing a plenary session, call Tel. 519.81.36)

A nymphlike statue modestly hiding among the leaves of Parc de Bruxelles

From the Palais de la Nation, cross the Koningsstraat, (the continuation of Rue Royale) and walk along Treurenberg. The Pléban Tower (another remnant of the fortifications) will be on your right, and the square towers of the Cathedral of St. Michel will be in front of you.

The Gothic **Cathedral of St.**

Michel is the national church of Belgium. The church is dedicated to St. Michel, patron of Brussels. The oldest parts were built in the 13th century, other parts were built in the 15th century and even later.

Armless and solemn – a statue at the Parc de Bruxelles

The **Cathedral Towers** are the work of Jan van Ruysbroeck, who also designed the Town Hall tower. The building, set at a busy traffic junction and somewhat faded by years of pollution, is still an imposing reminder of the Middle Ages. The towers are 226 feet tall, connected by a decoration of blind arches and niches. There is a statue of Saint Michel and a demon, and the huge portal at the center is decorated with statues of saints and historical Brabant figures. Begun in 1226 and finished over a span of two centuries, the architecture of the Cathedral covers the range of Gothic periods and ends with the Renaissance. Inside, its magnificence is multiplied: Roman columns, statues of the apostles, and richly stained glass windows. The high altar is decorated with embossed copper and the wood sculptures on the pulpit represent Adam and Eve being expelled from paradise.

The Chapelle de Saint-Sacrement, built between 1534 and 1539, is remarkable for its delicate stained glass windows. The stained glass of the Chapelle de Notre-Dame dates from 1656 and shows episodes in the life of the Virgin Mary.

St. Michel's was elevated to a Cathedral only in 1961; formerly it was Collegiate Church of Saint Michel and Saint Gudule. The carillon which has 49 bells was added in 1975. Tel. 217.83.45. Open 7am-6pm (winter) and 7am-7pm (summer). Visits to the crypt on request only.

Return to the Grand' Place along the Rue de la Montagne, which curves round to join the

Rue Marché aux Herbes. The square between these two streets is a meeting point for the youth of Brussels. This is the place to get a glimpse of future fringe fashions. Alternatively, you can follow the signs toward De Brouckère, center of the city, where large boulevards connecting the North and South Stations meet. Boulevard Anspach branches into Boulevards Emile Jacqmain and Adolphe Max.

Another alternative is to walk along Konings Straat, towards Place du Congrés. In the plaza is a column commemorating the National Congress, which in 1831, proclaimed the Belgian Constitution. At its foot burns the eternal flame, in honor of the unknown soldiers of the two world wars.

Place de l'Albertine

Old and New – From De Brouckère to Place Rogier

Metro: De Brouckère
Bus: 29, 63, 65, 66

De Brouckère is a commercial and entertainment center with shopping streets radiating out from it. From De Brouckère, go along Rue des Augustins and curve around Place du Samedi. You will come upon the **Tour Noire** (Black Tower) on your left, another remnant of the 12th century ramparts. Just in front of you is the **Church of Sainte Catherine**. This large building was built in 1854 in a mixture of styles. Unremarkable in itself, it contains a collection of paintings which are well worth seeing. (Tel. 513.34.81. Open 8am-5pm, until 6pm in summer. Closed Sunday afternoons).

In the morning a fruit and vegetable market is set up on the small square in front, but it is the great oblong **fish market** beside it that is really worth seeing. This is becoming a fashionable place to live. The square has been remodeled, and an elegant fountain was moved here from De Brouckère. The huge wheel of a drawbridge is embedded in concrete, a reminder that this was once a channel where fishing boats came in. The streets on either side, quai au Bois à Brûler and quai aux Briques, are lined with fish restaurants. Their menus are based on the day's catch, purchased at one of the fish markets a door or two away. The markets have retained their lovely old doorways and they are open daily from 7am-5pm. The restaurants here are at least comparable to those of the Ilot Sacré, from the luxurious *La Siréne d'Or* to simple and delicious *Chez Jacques*.

The Church of Sainte Catherine, reflected in various shades of green

Stand on the square at Rue Populier for a view of the **Church of Saint Jean Baptiste au Béguinage**. This church is a remarkable example of the 17th century Italo-Flemish baroque style. Its façade is considered one of the most beautiful in

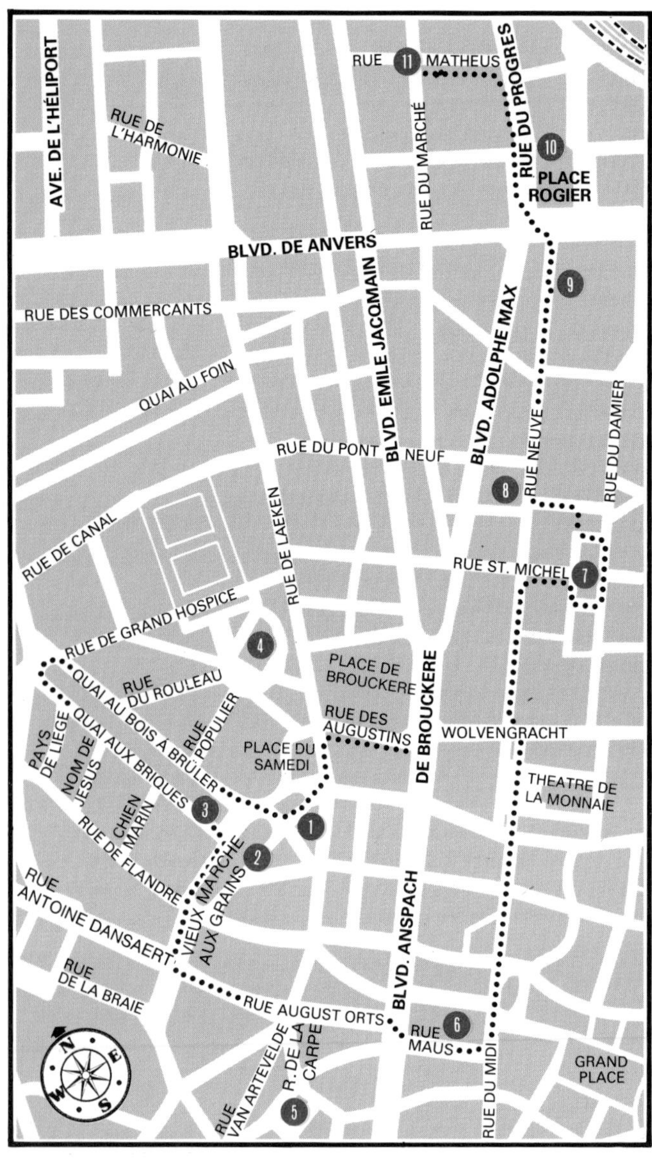

FROM DE BROUCKERE TO PLACE ROGIER

1. *Tour Noire*
2. *Church of Sainte-Catherine*
3. *Fish Market*
4. *Church of Saint Jean Baptiste au Béguinage*
5. *Marché St. Géry*
6. *Bourse*
7. *Place des Martyrs*
8. *Church of Notre-Dame de Finistère*
9. *City II*
10. *Centre Rogier*
11. *Red Light District*

Belgium. (Tel. 218.87.42. Open Sun.-Tues. 10am-5pm, Wed.-Fri. 9am-5pm. Closed on Mondays) The Beguinage itself, more of a hostel than a convent, for ladies who wished to retire from the world, was founded in 1250 and destroyed in the French Revolution.

You can then explore the streets near Sainte Catherine's church, where a number of old-fashioned shops make a delightful change from the usual boutiques. A favorite is the *Herboristerie et Droguerie Traditionnelle Desmecht*, across from the church, where all sorts of herbs and spices and Marseilles soap are sold. Further down, *Praslin* (on the Vieux Marché aux Grains) sells handmade chocolates.

The cross-street Rue de Flandre was the first commercial road between Cologne (Germany) and Bruges, and of course, the merchants stopped at the Brussels markets along the way. On the next street, there is the covered grain market, which dates back to the 1900's and which was abandoned for a time, but is now being restored as a market.

Rue Antoine has become a fashion street, a place where young Belgian designers are hanging out their wares at shops like *Sanz*, *Stijl*, *Khym,* and *Kat* for children.

The 17th century façade of the Church of Saint Jean Baptiste au Béguinage is considered one of the most beautiful in Belgium

Seafood – an eye-catching jumble of colors at the fish market

On your way to the Grand' Place you will see on your right the Marché St. Géry, at the end of the short Rue de la Carpe. Until recently a church, on the site where St. Gery built his chapel in the 6th century, in the earliest days on the Brussels development as a town, it is now a complex of small shops and coffee-houses.

Nearby on Rue Maus 2, is the Bourse, Brussels' exchange, which is housed in an impressive neoclassical building (See "Around the Grand' Place").

Stop off for a coffee or beer at *Falstaff*, Rue Maus 17. There is almost always a place to sit, even if you have to go to the back room. Admire the art nouveau as you settle down between young lovers and old folks playing cards.

After resting here for a while you can return to Grand' Place, or if you have the energy you can continue to an area with a different atmosphere. Turn left into Rue du Midi and proceed to Théâtre de la Monnaie. Cross over Place de la Monnaie to Rue Neuve.

This pedestrian mall is one of the busiest and most crowded in Brussels, and has some fine department stores. Off the Rue Neuve is the **Notre-Dame de Finistère**, from the early years of the 18th century, which contains a Madonna given by Scottish Roman Catholics of Aberdeen to the Infanta Isabella in 1625 (Tel. 217.52.52). Nearby, down Rue St. Michel, is the **Place des Martyrs**, a quiet and dignified square surrounded by uniform buildings designed in 1775 by Fisco. In the center of the square is the mass grave of the *Bruxellois* who died fighting for their independence against the Dutch in 1830.

At the end of Rue Neuve is **City II**, a huge shopping center containing shops, restaurants and eight movie theaters. However, the most elegant shops are across town, along Avenues Louise and de la Toison d'Or.

The **Centre Rogier** is a complex of 600 apartments, 350 offices and accommodation for fairs and exhibitions. The **Theatre National de Belgique** is also here.

From Place Rogier, it is a short hop to the North Station. One of the city's red-light districts lies between Rue du Progrès and Blvd. Jacqmain and behind the station. Here scantily-clad prostitutes sit in their "shop windows" along the streets.

The Centre Rogier houses 600 apartments as well as 350 offices and accommodation for fairs and exhibitions

Other Sites

Cinquantenaire

The 90-acre Parc Cinquantenaire lies outside the center of the city, but on a fine day it can be reached by walking down the Rue de la Loi. The triple **Triumphal Arch** will be your landmark. It was built in 1904-5 by Charles Giravit to commemorate Belgian independence. At Rond-point Schuman you will pass the **EEC Building**, Rue de la Loi 200. The building is shaped like a four-pointed star, and is often called the Berlaymont, after the monastery that used to be there.

The park itself was created in 1880 for the celebration of the 50th anniversary of Belgian independence. The Brussels Mosque and Islamic Cultural Center is in the northwest corner, and not far from there is a memorial, built in 1921, to the Belgian explorers and missionaries. The dominant feature of the park is the **Palais du Cinquantenaire**. Semicircular colonnaded wings lead up to a triumphal arch with a quadriga (Roman chariot) by Vincotte. On either side of it there are statues of women, nine in all, representing the provinces of Belgium – but Flanders got short shrift, with one statue representing two provinces.

Three of the city's best museums can be

Statuettes on the Triumphal Arch, which was built in 1904-5 to commemorate the independence of Belgium

The impressive Triumphal Arch at the Cinquantenaire Park

found here, one next to another: the Royal Museum of Art and History, the Royal Museum of the Army and Military History, and the new privately-owned *Autoworld*.

The **Musées Royaux d'Art et d'Histoire** (Royal Art and History Museum) Tel. 741.72.11. Entry free, is Open weekdays, except Mondays, 9:30am-5pm, Sat.-Sun. and public holidays from 10am.

On the even-numbered days of the month, you can see the ancient civilizations of Egypt, Greece, Rome, the Americas and the Near East. On odd-numbered days, the sections devoted to the decorative arts in Europe are open: study the tapestry, lace, stained glass, jewelry, ceramics and precision instruments. A neo-Gothic cloister of the museum houses a touch-museum for the blind, which has a Braille catalogue and taped commentaries. There is also a collection of old vehicles, including bicycles, and an exhibition of the history of glass, which has many superb and rare items.

An interesting item from the collection of old vehicles at the Royal Art and History Museum

The **Musée Royaux de l'Armée et d'Histoire Militaire** (Royal Museum of

Artillery on exhibit at the Royal Museum of the Army and Military History

the Army and Military History) has an astounding array of memorabilia, enriched by the many invasions of the country. (Tel. 733.44.93. Entry free. Open daily 9am-noon and 1-4:45pm. Closed Mon. and public holidays). In addition to weapons, artillery and uniforms, there are vehicles which were used in the First and Second World Wars, plus some 150 airplanes and balloons.

Autoworld claims the largest collection of vehicles in Europe, housed in what was originally an exhibition hall for auto shows. (Tel. 736.41.65. Admission fee. Open daily 10am-5pm; from April 1-Oct. 30 10am-6pm. Some 450 vehicles, including trucks and motorcycles, from 14 countries are on display, from Isettas to Cadillacs, from Hupmobiles to Whippets. The unique collection traces the history of automobiles from 1896. Many trademarks have since disappeared – Minerva, Imperia and Germain, for instance – but the cars are a touch of nostalgia for the past glory of the Belgian car industry. Here you can see cars that belonged to many famous and infamous men, such as John F. Kennedy's Cadillac and Hitler's armored Mercedes car. You can also see toys, posters, engravings, accessories, a library, videos and films. Receptions and dinners can be arranged after-hours in the museum's smaller rooms.

Tervuren Park – Out of the Crowded City

From the Cinquantenaire, it is a quarter-hour's tram ride (No. 44 to the end of the line) to **Tervuren Park** and the **Royal Museum of Central Africa** (Musée Royal d'Afrique Centrale). Leuvensesteenweg 13 Tervuren. Tel. 769.52.11. Admission fee. Open from March 16-Oct. 15 9am-5:30pm and from Oct. 16-March 15 10am-4:30pm. An elephant statue in front greets you. Built in 1905, the museum is a reduced copy of the Petit Palais in Paris. The museum is divided into Human Science and Natural Science. The **Human Science** section is devoted to the discovery, exploration and colonization of what was once the Belgian Congo (now Zaire). It covers prehistory, anthropology and ethnology. There is an interesting collection of primitive wood carvings, and a large collection of masks arranged according to regions. There is also a collection of musical instruments, a canoe capable of carrying up to 100 men, and a series of animal dioramas. The **Natural Science** section covers geology, mineralogy, paleontology and zoology.

The surrounding park is huge, it contains ornamental gardens, the baroque chapel of Saint-Hubert, said to occupy the spot where

Dolls at work at the Royal Art and History Museum

he died in 727, the stables of the 18th century castle of Charles of Lorraine, destroyed by fire, and the Gordael mill, all near the lakes.

Musée Horta

(Rue Americaine 25. Tel. 537.16.92. Open daily except Monday 2-5:30pm. Guided tours on request. Closed public holidays.) Although famous for its Old Masters and fine city square, Brussels is now also becoming increasingly celebrated as the birthplace of the turn-of-the-century architectural style, art nouveau, of which Victor Horta (1861-1947) was a leading practitioner. This style almost completely abolished the straight line, and used rich materials like marble, glass and wrought iron in new ways.

Art nouveau, a decorative art movement, began in Western Europe and lasted from the 1880's to World War I. It was characterized by richly ornamental, asymmetrical designs, often using motifs like flowers, twining plant tendrils and organic forms. Other major exponents of art nouveau in architecture, besides Victor Horta, were Henry van de Velde in Belgium, Hector Guimard in France, Antonio Gaudí in Spain, Peter Behrens in Germany and Louis Sullivan in the U.S.A. Art nouveau was also successfully expressed in furniture, jewelry, book design and illustration, by the illustrators Aubrey Beardsley and Walter Crane (England) and Otto Eckmann (Germany), the jewelry designer René Lalique (France), the painter Gustav Klimt (Austria) and the glassware designer Louis C. Tiffany (U.S.A.).

Listening to explanations on the ornate door at the Royal Art and History Museum

Lovers of this style should not miss the Horta Museum in the architect's former home. You can see Horta's masterpieces and his library, drawings, plans and photographs.

Horta became famous in his own lifetime for his designs. His masterpieces include Tassel House, Solvay House and Eetvelde House. Exponents of the style aimed to synthesize architecture with painting and sculpture, and to allow the artisans more individual expression. Horta and other art nouveau architects went against established norms and tried to suit housing to the needs of the individuals living and working within the building. For some time Brussels provided international inspiration for the art nouveau style, but the style was superseded by the emergence of new more modern styles.

The exquisite interior design of the Royal Art and History Museum

A walker's guide, published in English, Dutch and French enables the visitor to discover the best of art nouveau architecture within a single district of the city. The guide is on sale at the Tourist Information Office. Here you can also get information on guided tours conducted by various organisations.

Lakes and Forests – Ixelles and Bois de la Cambre

If you are exhausted from sightseeing, its time for a rest in a group of parks which have playgrounds, boating lakes, restaurants, jogging trails, golf courses and two race tracks.

Taking a break

Start at the two ponds of **Ixelles**, all that remain of a string of ponds along the Maelbeek Valley. Their banks have been "arranged", but they are large and pleasant. Just past them is the **Abbey de la Cambre**. The monastery was founded in 1196 by the Sisters of the Cistercian Order. Most of the building which we see today was rebuilt in the 17th and 18th centuries, because the building was seriously damaged during the Wars of

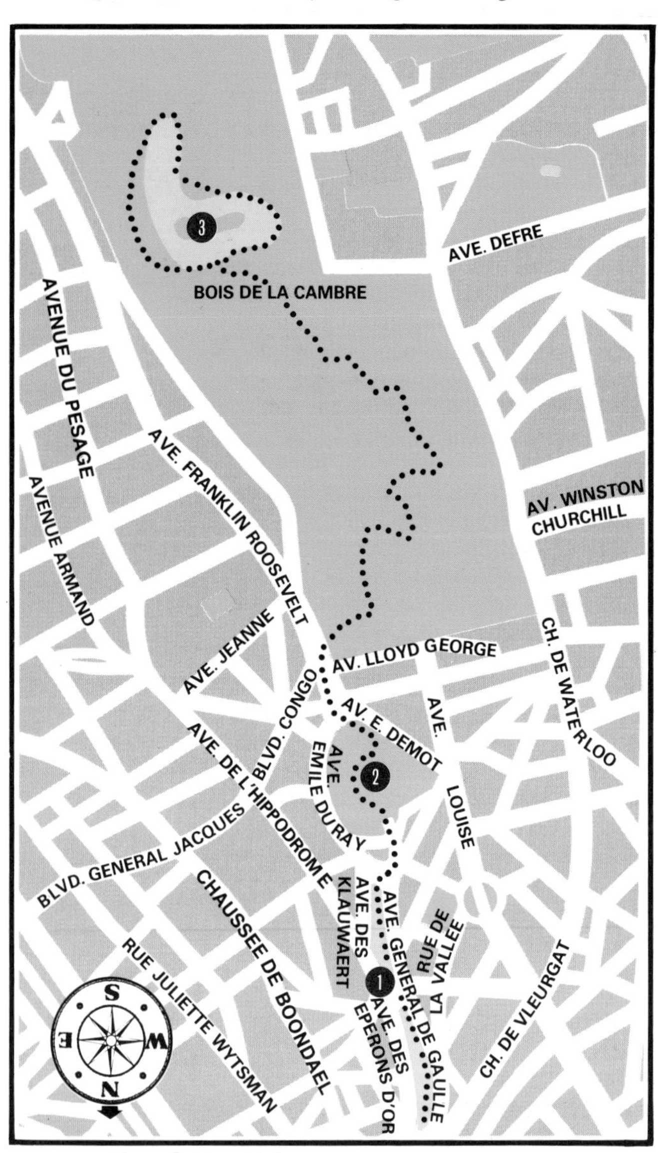

IXELLES AND BOIS DE LA CAMBRE

1. Ponds of Ixelles
2. Abbey de la Cambre
3. "Robinson" Island

Religion. Only the church itself is from the 14th century. Nearby is a cloister from the 16th century which was reconstructed in the 1930's. The abbey is one of five in Brussels, whose grounds join the Bois de la Cambre. (Tel. 648.11.21. Open daily 9am-noon, 3-6pm; Sat. 3-6pm, Sun. 9am-12:30pm).

Capturing the magical moments on film

Just south of the monastery is **Bois de la Cambre**. To reach this forest you must go up from the valley and turn left into Avenue de Mot. This leads to Avenue Franklin Roosevelt, which you should follow a short distance until you see the forest on your right. Several roads and many footpaths cross the forest, so you can turn in at the first one you find.

The forest, which was once part of Forét de Soignes, was bought in the 19th century by the city of Brussels and given its present form. The forest has outstanding landscapes in all seasons of the year, but autumn is perhaps the most beautiful, when the trees are covered in leaves of autumnal shades. Here you will find paths where you can walk, run or ride, a number of coffee shops and restaurants, and even a lake with the small "Robinson" island which you can reach in a small ferry. The path around the lake is very popular with joggers and people walking their dogs. This landscaped park in turn connects with the 10,000-acre Foret de Soignes, a beech forest which stretches all the way to Waterloo.

Laeken – Eclectic Architecture

On the northern edge of Brussels lies another green space, **Laeken**. On our way there from the city center, we will probably be surprised by the Gothic church which looms above as we leave the tunnel. This is **Eglise Notre-Dame de Laeken**. The church was built in 1817 and was dedicated to

Louise Marie the first Queen of the Belgians. The church contains the tombs of Leopold I, Leopold II, Albert I and Queen

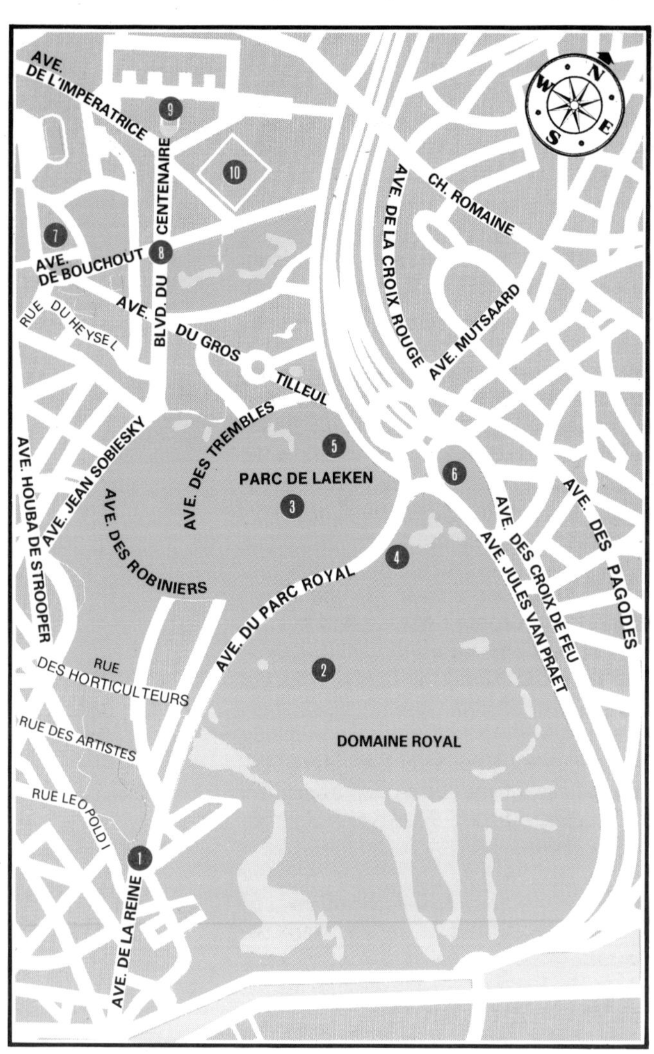

LAEKEN

1. Église Notre-Dame de Laeken
2. Royal Palace
3. Leopold I Monument
4. Royal Greenhouse
5. Villa Belvédère
6. Chinese Pavilion
7. Planétarium
8. Atomium
9. Palais du Centenaire
10. Trade Mart Building

Brussels' Planetarium

Astrid. (Tel. 426.87.68. Open first Sunday April to October 3-5pm).

The road goes round Domaine Royale. Further on you will see on the right the fence of the **Royal Palace** in which the royal family lives today. It is not possible to visit the palace, so we can only catch a glimpse through the fence. The palace was built in 1784 by the Austrian governors of Belgium in Louis XVI style. Napoleon also spent some time here, and organised renovations in 1802, and it was here that he gave the order to invade Russia. Although the palace itself is not open to the public, for a few days in May it is possible to visit the **Royal Greenhouse** which is an integral part of the royal estate. The Royal Greenhouse contains a rather large collection of exotic flowers.

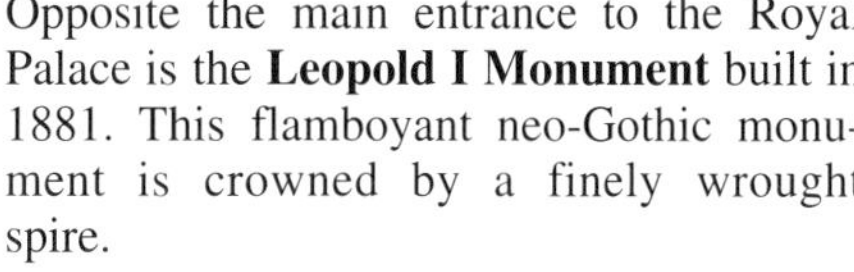

Opposite the main entrance to the Royal Palace is the **Leopold I Monument** built in 1881. This flamboyant neo-Gothic monument is crowned by a finely wrought spire.

Also in this park is the **Villa Belvédère**, residence of the heir to the throne (today the King's brother Prince Albert and his wife Princess Paola).

At the end of Avenue du Parc Royal and not far from the Belvedere is the **Neptune Fountain**, a copy of the 16th century work by Jean de Bologne (Giambologna) which stands in Bologna, Italy.

Two Oriental jewels were erected in the park at the whim of King Leopold II, who bought a **Japanese Tower** and a **Chinese Pavilion** at the Paris Exhibition of 1900 and brought them home. (Ave. Van Praet 44. Tel. 268.16.08. Entry free. Open daily 10am-4:45pm. Closed Mon.). The pavilion contains a fine collection of 17th and 18th century Chinese porcelain.

Across the park is the **Planétarium**. (Tel. 478.95.26. Ave. de Bouchout 10. Admission fee. The timetable changes, so check with the tourist office.) It boasts a complicated optical projection system which can show the sky in all its starry splendor to a roomful of people.

The Planetarium, however, is overshadowed in size and popularity by the **Atomium**, which rivals even the Manneken-Pis as symbol of the city. (Heysel, Blvd. du Centenaire. Tel. 477.09.77. Admission fee. Open daily 10am-6pm. The Panorama is open Sept.-March, 10am-6pm, April-June 10am-8pm.) Built for the 1958 World's Fair, this 335 ft. aluminium structure represents a molecule of an iron crystal magnified 265 million times. The three lower spheres of the nine "atoms" house exhibitions on the peaceful use of nuclear energy, and the top sphere is a restaurant with a panorama platform. They are connected by escalators and elevators running through 20 tubes. The exhibition inside the spheres is somewhat disappointing.

A visit to Bruparck, an amusement park by the Atomium

At the foot of the Atomium is **Bruparck,** an amusement park offering plenty of fun. Among its facilities is Mini-Europe, a lovely park with over 300 models of famous buildings; Kinepolis – a cinema complex with 24 theatres and an Imax theater with a 600 sq/m screen; the Océade, with swimming pools and water slides. (Tel. 477.03.77. Open from April to December).

Nearby is the Heysel, the exposition park complex begun for the 1935 Universal Exhibition, and stretching out to include the **Palais du Centenaire**, where 100 years of Belgian independence was commemorated.

The complex has been enlarged several times; the Central Hall is an attractive example of modern architecture.

To the side is the huge **International Trade Mart Building**, built in 1975 by the American architect John Portman. It contains a permanent exhibition of Belgian-made products, open only to wholesalers.

Anderlecht

An easy visit of varied interest is the trip to Anderlecht, near the end of the Metro line (use the Saint-Guidon stop). Within a small area are Erasmus' House, the Church of Saint Peter and Saint Guidon, and an old Beguinage.

At Rue de Chapitre 31, you can see the house where the Dutch humanist philosopher **Erasmus** lived in 1521. (Tel. 521.13.83. Tram 103. Bus 47 or 49. Metro to Saint-Guidon. Admission fee. Open 10am-noon and 2-5pm. Closed Tuesday, Friday and Jan. 1). The house has been turned into a museum containing his books, engravings showing him on his travels and a copy of Holbein's portrait of him.

The **Church of St Peter and St Guidon**, at Place de la Vaillance, contains the remains of Saint Guidon, who is the patron of farm animals. Built in the 14th to 16th centuries, with a Romanesque crypt, it contains a rare tombstone dating from the 11th or 12th century. (Tel. 521.84.15. Open daily 9am-noon and 2:30-6pm, closed on Sun. during services).

The **Béguinage** dates from 1252, and is worth while visiting to see how pious women withdrew from society without going into a convent.

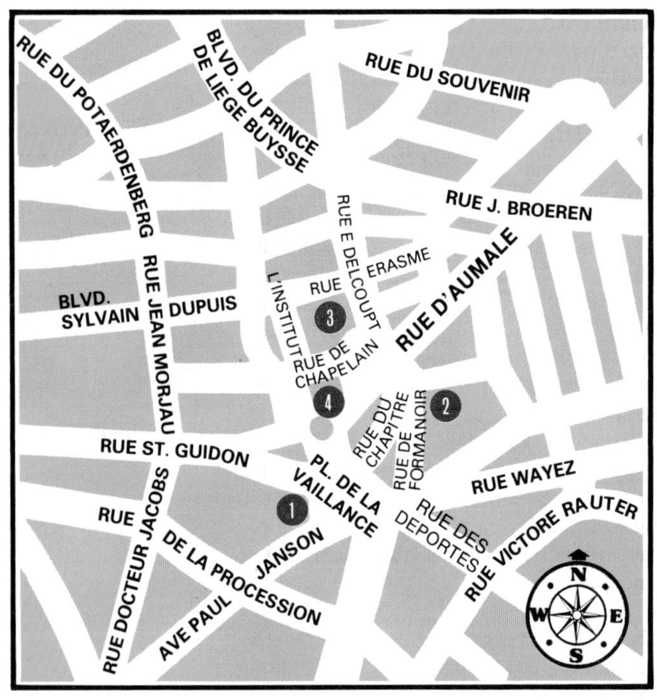

ANDERLECHT

1. Metro
2. Erasmus Museum
3. Beguinage
4. Church of St. Peter

Waterloo

So far, we have remained within the city, but history and war buffs may wish to make the short trip to Waterloo, where the Duke of Wellington defeated Napoleon on June 18, 1815.

Guided tours are available, from a quick look at the museums and monuments to an all-day exploration of the battlefield, which stretches from the town Waterloo to Genappe and from Plancenoit to Braine-l'Alleud.

Almost every visitor ascends the 226 steps up an artificial, conical knoll to the **Lion**

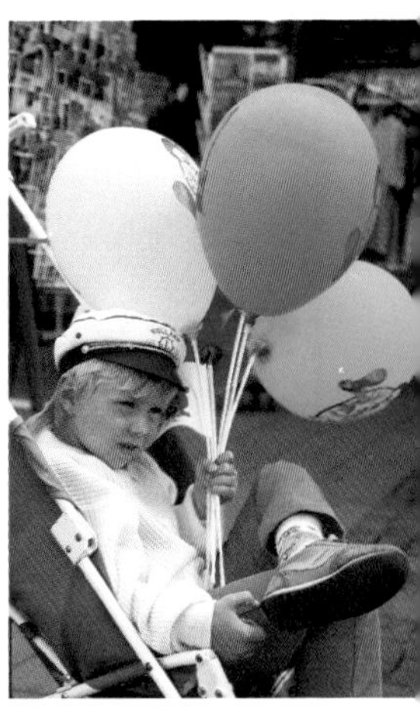

Monument. From the summit, there is a superb view of the plain where Wellington and Blucher defeated Napoleon. It can be climbed 9am-6:30pm from April to October. Tel. 384.31.39.

In 1824 the women of Liege built the knoll, which is over 120 feet high, by carrying the soil in baskets on their backs. The lion symbolizes the victors, England and the Netherlands. The lion monument was built by the government of the United Netherlands on the spot where the Prince of Orange was wounded. From the monument it is possible to see most of the places of importance in the battlefield. The monument itself was created by the sculptor Van Geel in cast iron. Around the foot of the mound there are cafés and souvenir shops, plus a panorama of the battlefield and a museum.

Other monuments and sites include the French monument "Aigle Blessé", the monuments to the Belgians, the Prussians and the Hanoverians, Napoleon's observation post, two farms (rebuilt) "Haie Sainte" and "La Belle Alliance", and the Victor Hugo Column.

The **Wellington Museum** is located in a former inn, which was the Duke's rear headquarters where he spent two nights preceding the battle. (Chaussée de Bruxelles 147. Tel. 354.78.06. Admission fee. Open 9:30am-6:30pm from April 1-Nov. 15, 10:30am-5pm from Nov. 16-March 31).

An illuminated map lets you follow the progress of the battle, through each stage. Separate rooms are devoted to the nations which took part in the battle, and there is also a room devoted to the history of Waterloo village.

The **Musée Provincial du Caillow** (Napoleonic Museum) is likewise the site where Napoleon and his staff spent the night before the battle. (Chaussée de Bruxelles 66, Vieux-Genappe. Tel. 384.24.24. Admission fee. Open 10am-6:30pm April 1-Oct. 31; 1:30-5pm Nov. 1-March 31; closed Mondays and all of January.) The museum contains Napoleon's death mask. A rotunda houses Louis Dumoulin's panoramic painting *The Battlefield on the Evening of June 18, 1815*.

Walibi

20 kms south-east of Brussels is Walibi, an amusement park with many attractions, including shows, rides and river adventures. **Aqualibi** deserves a special mention. This is a tropical park with water attractions such as a wave pool and jet stream.

To reach Walibi, take the E411 (Brussels-Namur), exit 6 (Wavre); train: line Ottignies – Louvain-la-Neuve, Bierges station. Tel. (010)41.44.66. Admission fee. Open April-September 10am-6pm. Aqualibi is also open in the winter, 2-10pm, but is closed on Mondays all year round (except during school holidays). During the summer Aqualibi is reserved for visitors of Walibi only.

"MUSTS" IN BRUSSELS

For those who have only a few days in Brussels, and who are dazzled by the wealth of attractions available, we have listed a few sites below without which no visit to the city is complete.

Grand' Place and Hôtel de Ville: In the heart of Brussels, Grand' Place is one of the most beautiful squares in Europe, dominated by the Hôtel de Ville (Town Hall), a Gothic masterpiece. Hôtel de Ville is open October-March 9:30am-12:15pm, 1:45-4pm; April-Sept. 9:30am-5pm; Sun. and public holidays 10am-noon, 2-4pm. Tel. 512.75.54. Guided tours except when the City Council is in session (see "Grand' Place – The Crowning Jewel").

Musées Royaux des Beaux-Arts de Belgique (The Royal Museums of Fine Arts): It has separate galleries for Ancient and Modern Art, and an outstanding collection of art, especially Flemish art. Rue de la Regence 3. Tel. 507.82.00. Open 10am-noon, 2-5pm. Entry free (see "Art and Royalty – Mont des Arts to the Cathedral").

At the Royal Art and History Museum

Manneken-Pis: The famous statue has become a symbol of the free spirit of Brussels. Rue de l'Etuve, near the corner of Rue de Chene (see "Around the Grand' Place").

Musées Royaux d'Art et d'Histoire (The Royal Art and History Museum): A museum with exhibits from ancient civilizations and decorative arts in Europe. In Parc Cinquantenaire. Tel. 741.72.11. Open Tues.-Fri. 9:30am-5pm. Sat., Sun. and public holidays from 10am. Entry free (see "Other Sites – Cinquantenaire").

Sablon: A district of art galleries, with a garden and antique market. Between Place Royale and Palais de Justice. (see "Antiques and Flea Markets – From Sablon to Place du Jeu de Balle").

Cathedral of St. Michel: The national church of Belgium, built in Gothic style with remarkable stained glass windows, and rich in history and art. Near the Central Station. Tel. 217.83.45. Open 7am-7pm (summer), 7am-6pm (winter), (see "Art and Royalty – Mont des Arts to the Cathedral").

Musée Royal de l'Armée et d'Histoire Militaire (Royal Museum of the Army and Military History): An amazing collection of military memorabilia, from uniforms and weapons to aircrafts. In Parc Cinquantenaire. Open daily except Mondays 9am-noon and 1-4:45pm. Closed public holidays, entry free (see "Other Sites – Cinquantenaire").

Exhibits at the Royal Museum of Army and Military History

MAKING THE MOST OF YOUR STAY

Wining and Dining

The Belgians demand both quality and quantity, and they demand good presentation as well. This is the place to find first-class seafood (steamed mussels, tiny shrimps and baby eels), and the beefsteaks are also good. *Waterzooi*, perhaps best described as a thick, white stew, made with chicken or fish, is a specialty. Asparagus

is a favorite with many chefs. *Boudin*, the national sausage, appears in several varieties and the famous Ardennes ham is found almost everywhere. In season, game is popular. As for cheese, some of the best are Trappist cheeses similar to Port-Salut and the soft but strong Brussels cheese.

Breads vary from place to place, but the most typical Belgian bread is the sweet *pain à la grecque*. It has nothing to do with Greece: the name comes from the bread that the monks used to give to the poor.

Brussels' waffles, called *gaufres*, taste best when freshly baked in the iron at a street-side stand. In cafés, they come with a variety of toppings. There are cream cakes and sugar tarts, and the Brussels chocolates have a reputation around the world. You can find the handmade ones in luxury shops – *Godiva*, *Côte d'Or*, *Neuhaus* and *Corne de la Toison d'Or*. *Leonidas* is the cheaper machine-made chocolate, quite popular nonetheless.

The fried potato is a national institution. City streets and country roads are lined with *frites* stands, and even the Dutch (who actually eat more fries than their next-door neighbors) laugh about the Belgians' insatiable appetite for the potato.

Paul Ilegems, professor at Antwerp's Royal Academy of Fine Arts, sees the *frites* stand

Brussels' waffles taste best when freshly baked in an iron and served with a variety of toppings

An appetizing array of seafood

as "a symbol of the Belgian character – a spirit of improvisation, liberty, even anarchy. The owner makes the stand as he wants it, with few laws to tell him what to do. He is a free spirit. I see the *frites* stand as a kind of folk art".

Frites stands – called *frituur* in Flemish and *friterie* in the French-speaking regions – are accessible and inexpensive. They are generally open mid-afternoon to midnight or later. Traditional paper cones are giving way to flat cardboard or plastic serving dishes, even though the cones seem more

practical, absorbing excess grease, keeping the *frites* hot longer and allowing them to drain better. A wide variety of sauces can be ordered with *frites*, although originally they were served only with salt.

Belgium has little wine of its own, as its vineyards were destroyed in World War I and the industry never picked up again. Nevertheless, fine wines are available from its neighbors; France, Luxembourg and Germany. An effort has been made to introduce wine from the country's famous hothouse grapes, grown around Houlat and Overijse, but the quantities are limited.

The Belgians drink red or white *porto* as an aperitif, but beer is far and away the most popular drink. The beer menu in a pub can be more extensive than the wine card in many a restaurant.

Restaurants

Brussels is considered the best place in Europe for fine cuisine. The city has over 1500 restaurants, and the quality of the dishes they offer is superb. Brussels is regarded as the main center of French cuisine, after Lyons. Local specialities include *Faisan à la Brabançonne* (pheasant with chicory), *Lapin à la Bière* (rabbit with beer), eels, and mussels. Desserts and pastries are also outstanding, many are based on chocolate.

The visitor to Brussels will have no difficulty in finding a good restaurant where he can enjoy excellent food and presentation. A major concentration of good restaurants – generally expensive – is found in Grand' Place and the vicinity, especially the area of **Ilot Sacré**, just north of the Grand' Place. Here you can find restaurants of every kind: seafood, Greek, Chinese, Spanish, and of course French.

Another concentration of restaurants is found around **Ste. Catherine square**, west of De Broukére. This is the place to come for seafood.

If you simply want something light, there is an abundance of inexpensive fast food places. For a light meal there are also many reasonable restaurants such as *Pizzaland*, which are easy to find wherever you go. Another interesting possibility is a restaurant where you cook your own food! This you can do at *Maison d'Attila*, Avenue du Prince de Ligne 36-44, Tel. 375.38.05.

Consult the T.I.B for an issue of their "Gourmet Guide" which includes listings of restaurants.

The following are some of Brussels' favorite restaurants. Price is per person for a meal, without drinks.

CRÈME DE LA CRÈME
Barbizon: Welriekendedreef

Seafood arranged in splendid decor

95. Tel. 657.04.62. Closed Tuesday, Wednesday and throughout February.

Bruneau: Ave. Broustin 73-75. Tel. 427.69.78. Closed Tuesday evening, Wednesday, Thursday and public holidays.

Comme Chez Soi: Place Rouppe 23. Tel. 512.29.21. The critics agree that it's the best in Brussels. Closed Sunday, Monday, Christmas to the New Year.

Claude-Dupont: Ave. Vital-Riethuisen 46. Tel. 426.00.00. Closed Monday, Tuesday and mid-July to mid-August.

L'Ecailler du Palais Royal: Rue Bodenbroek 18. Tel. 512.87.51. Closed Sunday, holidays and late July to early September.

Le Sermon: Ave. Jacques-Sermon 91. Tel. 426.89.35. Closed Sunday, Monday and July.

Les Baguettes Imperiales: Ave. J. Sobieski 70. Tel. 479.67.32.

Closed Sunday evening, Tuesday, and August.

La Maison du Cygne: Grand' Place 9. Tel. 511.82.44. Closed Saturday noon, Sunday, Aug. 10-17 and Christmas season. One of the best restaurant in Brussels with a less formal restaurant downstairs.

Oasis: Place Marie-José 9. Tel. 648.45.45. Closed Sunday and first part of August.

La Sirène d'Or: Place Sainte-Catherine 1A. Tel. 513.51.98. Closed Sunday, Monday and July.

Villa d'Este: Rue de l'Etoile 142. Tel. 376.48.48. Closed Sunday evening, Monday, August and Christmas to New Year's Day.

DELUXE RESTAURANTS

Astrid "Chez Pierrot": Rue de la Presse 21. Tel. 217.38.31. Closed Sunday.

Bernard: Rue Namur 93. Tel. 512.88.21. Closed Sunday, Monday evening and July.

Coq en Pâte: Rue Tomberg 259. Tel. 762.19.71. Closed Monday and August.

Huitrière: Quai aux Briques 20. Tel. 512.26.99.

Le Meiser: Blvd. Gen-Wahis 55. Tel. 735.37.69. Closed Saturday and Sunday.

La Porte des Indes: Ave. Louise 455. Tel. 640.30.59. Indian food. Closed Sunday.

Prince d'Orange: Ave. Prince-d'Orange 1. Tel. 374.48.71. Closed Monday.

Les Quatre Saisons (Royal Windsor Hôtel): Rue Duquesnoy 5. Tel. 505.51.00.

VERY GOOD RESTAURANTS

L'Amadeus: Rue Veydt 13. Tel. 538.34.27. Closed Monday.

Aux Armes de Bruxelles: Rue des Bouchers 13. Tel. 511.55.98. Closed Monday and last half of June.

La Belle Maraichere: Place Sainte Catherine 11. Tel. 512.97.59. Closed Wednesday till Thursday.

Buffet Primeur: Rue du Marché-aux-Herbes 78-80. Tel. 511.56.93. Buffet. Unlimited serving for a set price. Highly recommended.

Café D'Egmont (Hotel Hilton): Blvd. de Waterloo 38. Tel. 504.11.11. View of the park.

Coffre à Farine: Ave. du Bois de la Cambre 17A. Tel. 675.22.73. Closed Monday.

Café Henry: Rue de Laken 30. Tel. 219.64.45. Jazz on weekends, buffet at noon.

Casa Manuel: Grand Place 34. Tel. 511.47.47. Excellent Spanish food.

François: Quai aux Briques 2. Tel. 511.60.89. Closed Monday and in June.

Restaurant Jacques: Quai aux Briques 44. Tel. 513.27.62. Closed Sunday and holidays.

Chez Lagaffe: Rue de l'Epée 4. Tel. 511.76.39. Closed Sat. (noon) and Sunday.

Le Marmiton: Rue des Bouchers 43. Tel. 511.70.10.

Ogenblik: Galerie des Princes 1. Tel. 511.61.51. Closed Sunday.

La Villette: Rue du Vieux Marché aux Grains 3. Closed Sunday and July.

Vincent: Rue des Dominicains 8-10. Tel. 511.23.03. Closed August.

Enjoy one of the Grand' Place's inviting cafés

The art of smiling and pouring a beer

RESTAURANTS WORTH A TRIP OUT OF TOWN

Aloyse Kloos: Terhulpseskeenweg 2, Hoeilaart. Tel. 657.37.37. Closed Sunday evening, Monday and February.

Bellemolen: Statiestraat 11, Essene. Tel. 053.666.238. Closed Sunday evening and Monday, July, Christmas to New Year.

De Bijgaarden: Van Beverenstraat 20, Groot-Bijgaarden. Tel. 466.44.85. Closed Saturday afternoon and Sunday, end of April and last half of August.

Michel: Gossetlaan 31, Groot-Bijgaarden. Tel. 466.65.91. Closed Sunday, Monday and August.

Romeyer: Chaussée de Groenendael 109, Groenendael. Tel. 657.05.81. Closed Sunday evening, Monday and February.

Entertainment

Theater or night club, jazz or dancing, or just a movie (shown in original language with subtitles) – there is no lack of entertainment in Brussels.

The tourist office runs a telephone **reservation service** for the theater – TELETIB – that allows anyone with a European bank account to pay automatically through that account. Tel. 513.83.20. If you do not have a European bank account, you can make reservations at the Brussels Tourist Office (T.I.B.) in the Town Hall on Grand' Place. Open daily 11am-5pm. Every two months the T.I.B publishes a detailed agenda of all events: "Key to Brussels".

The **Théâtre Royal de la Monnaie** (Opera House) reopened in late 1986 after a complete renovation, which makes it one of the most modern and dramatic opera houses in Europe. The rather mundane exterior has two extra levels on top. The interior is a startling mixture of old and new. The floor of the entrance has geometric designs in black and white, and the ceiling has cheerful splashes of color. Both were the work of American artists: Sol Lewitt designed the floor and Sam Francis, the ceiling. Daniel Buren, who designed the inner court of the Palais Royale in Paris, added the black and white striped pillars at either end. The only thing that remains from the old rococo entrance are four angels in the stairway niches.

The Grand Foyer upstairs, where one can get a drink at intermission, has not been changed. The floor is parquet, the decor is rococo, and the original ceiling in the main dome has been restored. Backstage, there is a new mechanical system and one of the most sophisticated sound systems in the world. Tel. 218.12.11 Open Mon.-Sat. 11am-6pm. Closed July 2-August 19. For reservations call Tel. 217.22.11.

Brussels boasts six opera houses, ballet and concerts, and another three dozen theaters. Listings of shows are available from the tourist offices or can be found in the newspapers.

Jazz is a favorite among *Bruxellois*, and many cafés and restaurants have jazz dinners on Friday or jazz brunches on weekends.

JAZZ CLUBS

Bièrodrome: Place Fernand Cocq 21. Tel. 512.04.56.

Brussels Jazz Club: Grand' Place 13. Tel. 512.40.93.

Café Henry: Rue de Lahen 30. Tel. 219.69.45.

Chez Lagaffe: Rue de l'Epée 4. Tel. 511.76.39.

Clin d'Oeil: Rue Sainte-Anne 26. Tel. 513.50.36.

Epistrophy: Blvd.Leopold II 170. Tel. 428.38.65.

Planet: Borgval 14-20:16, Tel. 513.63.14.

Travers: Rue Traversière 11, Tel. 218.40.86.

Studio D.E.S.: Rue aux Fleurs 14, Tel. 217.24.20.

Vieux Bruxelles: Rue Ste. Catherine 23, Tel. 511.14.00.

COCKTAIL BARS

Bar Hotel Astoria: Rue Royale 103.

Big Apple: Ave. Louise 191.

La Brouette: Grand' Place 2.

Le Cerf: Grand' Place 20.

La Chaloupe d'Or: Grand' Place 24.

L'Imaginaire: Rue des Dominicains 24.

La Malcour: Place du Grand Sablon 18.

Métropole: Place de Brouckère 31.

Le Waterloo: Blvd. de Waterloo 59.

Le Wine Bar: Rue des Pigeons 9.

Brain Trust: Rue de Livourne 89.

Vol de Nuit: Rue du Magistrat 33.

CAFÉ-THEATERS

Escapade: Chaussée de Haecht 295. Tel. 242.33.71.

Etc.: Rue de la Poste 226. Tel. 214.35.03.

Les Jardins Suspendus: Rue Léon Théodor 110. Tel. 427.25.18.

La Soupape: Rue A. De-Witte 26. Tel. 649.58.88.

Ti Roro: Rue de la Sablonnière 26. Tel. 219.22.95.

DINNER-SHOWS OR MUSIC
Adagio: Rue de l'Epée 26. Tel. 511.79.03.

Le Beau Bruxell: Blvd. Baudouin 19. Tel. 217.12.87.

Le Black Bottom: Rue du Lombard 1. Tel. 511.06.08.

Bleu Cabaret: Blvd. Adolphe Max 184. Tel. 513.41.92.

Chez Flo: Rue au Beurre 25. Tel. 512.94.96.

El Rincon: Rue Haute 403. Tel. 538.38.46.

Le Pré Salé: Rue de Flandre 20. Tel. 513.43.23.

Rôtisserie du Danube: Blvd. Jacqmain 104. Tel. 217.45.48.

Le Slave: Rue Scailquin 22. Tel. 217.66.56.

Robin Hood: Salle King Richard, Rue Jourdan 13. Tel. 538.13.63.

En Plein Ciel: (Hilton Hotel), Blvd. de Waterloo 38. Tel. 513.88.77.

Garden Restaurant: (Ramada Hotel), Chausseé de Charleroi 38. Tel. 539.30.00.

Le Pavillon: (Sheraton Hotel), Place Rogier 3. Tel. 219.34.00.

BISTROS
Ballon Nord: Rue de Brabant 24. For those who like billiards.

La Bécasse: Rue Tabora 11.

Bistrot du Théâtre: Place Rogier 1. For the theater crowd.

Au Bon Vieux Temps: Impasse Saint-Nicolas, reached from Rue du Marche-aux-Herbes 12.

Cirio: Rue de la Bourse 18. Tel. 512.13.95 Especially interesting decor.

Falstaff: Rue Maus 17. Tel. 511.87.89 Lovely 1900 decor.

La Fleur en Papier doré: Rue des Alexiens 53. Surrealistic decor.

Goupil le Fol: Rue de la Violette 22. For Francophiles. Tel. 511.13.96.

Le Jugement Dernier: Chaussée de Haecht 165. Fantastic beer selection.

La Lunette: Place de la Monnaie 3. Tel. 218.03.78. Another great beer bar.

La Mort Subite: Rue Montagne-aux-Herbes-Potagères 7. Tel. 513.13.18.

't Spinnekopke: Place du Jardin-aux-Fleurs 1.

Brussels is famous for its wonderful chocolates

Taverniers: Rue Paul Devaux 12. Original 18th-century café with tea dances every afternoon.

Toone VII: Impasse Schuddeveld. Also a marionette theater. Tel. 511.71.37.

La Violette: Rue de la Violette 26. Selection of unusual beers.

Le Claridge: Chaussée de Louvain 24. A throwback to the '50's.

AMERICAN BARS AND ENGLISH PUBS

Corkscrew: Ave. d'Auderghem 17.

Le Montana: Chaussée de Waterloo 508.

Le Rainbow: Rue Léopold 7.
Rick's: Ave. Louise 344.

DISCOS

Les Caves de la Chapelle: Place de la Chapelle 6.

Le Circus: Chaussée de Saint-Job 10.

Crocodile Club: Rue Duquesnoy 7.

Le Dallas Club: Blvd. du Jardin Botanique 56.

Les Enfants Terribles: Ave. de la Toison d'Or 44.

Funny Horse: Rue de Livourne 37.

Dining in one of Brussels' many fine restaurants

La Gaiete: Rue Fosse-aux-Loups 18.

Les Minimes: Rue des Minimes 57.

Le Mirano: Chaussée de Louvain 38.

Pastel: Rue Berckmans 10.

Le Pied: Ave. Fraiteur 28.

Theatro: Rue Fosse-aux-Loups 18.

Le Vaudeville: Rue de la Montagne 14. (Fri. and Sun. only).

Le Variete: Rue Marché-aux-Porcs 11.

LATE-NIGHT RESTAURANTS

Le Loup Voyant: Ave. de la Couronne 562. Tel. 640.02.08.

Le Grande Porte: Rue Notre-Seigneur 9. Tel. 512.89.98.

Le Macon: Rue Joseph Stallaert 87. Tel. 344.84.87.

La Panthére: Rue de Joncker 39. Tel. 538.48.77.

Picotin: Ave. de la Couronne 443. Tel. 649.07.74.

Le Campus: Ave. de la Couronne 437. Tel. 648.53.80.

Le Celestin: Rue du Chatelain 10. Tel. 646.34.85.

Café de Paris: Rue de la Vierge Noire 12. Tel. 512.19.40.

Le Mozart: Chaussée d'Alsemberg 541. Tel. 344.08.09.

Festivals and Events

Brussels is a city where people know how to enjoy themselves. There is always something going on, somewhere. Here is a list of some events:

May (last weekend) – jazz Rally.

June – Brussels 20km race.

July – Historic procession in Grand' Place.

August – flower carpet in Grand' Place (every two years).

August – Brossella international folk and jazz festival.

Filling the Basket: Where to Shop and for What

It is only natural that the capital of Europe should be a cornucopia of goods from all over the world. Here you can find almost every luxury that you can find in other capital cities of Europe, and a lot more besides. Visitors should remember that foreigners can get a tax refund on any purchase costing 3500 francs or more (see "Practical Tips – VAT").

A large variety of newspapers, magazines and cards for sale on the street

Shopping in Brussels can be an exciting experience and can suit every pocket. You can choose between shops and galeries where you can find some of the best-known fashion names, or strolling between stalls in one of the many flea markets in Brussels, or if you prefer, you can go to one of the standard stores which are generally very elegant. Shopping, like most other things in Brussels, can be a very special aesthetic experience, and one you should not miss.

Luxury shops

The center of luxury shopping in Brussels is at and near **Place Louise**, and it includes Avenue Louise and Boulevard de Waterloo. Not far from the Place you will find *Galerie Louise*, the center for luxury and expensive shops. The *galerie* consists of a series of shops in a covered arcade – which makes it possible to shop in comfort even on the coldest or wettest days in winter. Here you can find mainly exclusive fashion shops, but also other shops besides. Of course, you will be able to have a light meal or a cup of coffee at one of the restaurants or cafés here.

Moderately priced shops

If you prefer to shop in less expensive centers, you will find many reasonably priced stores along **Rue Neuve**. In addition to many shops, you will also find a few department stores here, such as *Sarma* and *Marks and Spencer*. Everything is displayed most elegantly, and you can find almost anything you want. The main focal point of this area is the lovely *City II* shopping center, which has shops of every kind, cinemas, cafés and restaurants.

Specialty shops

Several areas in Brussels specialize in particular types of shops.

Antiques: The center for antique buying and selling in Brussels is in Place du Grand Sablon.

Lace: Belgian lace is famous for its quality. There are many lace shops in Rue de l'Etuve which leads from the Grand' Place to the Manneken-Pis. There you can find lace of different kinds, sizes and qualities, for different purposes, from tablecloths, napkins and curtains to bookmarkers.

Jewelry: There are many places to buy jewelry all over Brussels, but there is a concentration of jewelry stores in the area between the Grand' Place and the Bourse.

Gazing at a lovely display of Brussels' famous lace

Crystal: A gallery specializing in Belgian crystal is *Art Selection*, located in Marché-aux-Herbes 83, near the Grand' Place.

Books: Bookstores are found all over town, but a concentration of bookstores is found along Boulevard Adolphe Max. Here you will find *Smith & Son*, which sells mainly English books.

Chocolates: The world-famous Belgian chocolates are found almost everywhere in Brussels, and visitors probably need little encouragement to taste them. A gift of Belgian chocolates is always a good idea. We will mention just a few of the well-known manufacturers: *Godiva*, *Léonidas*, *Côte d'Or*, *Neuhaus* and *Corne de la Toison d'Or*.

At the flower market

Late-night shops

There are many late-night shops in Brussels, selling anything from groceries to tobacco and books. Most are concentrated north of the Grand' Place, and are open daily between midnight and 3am. Some stores have a delivery service.

Grand' Place Store: Rue de la Colline 7. Tel 512.86.87.

The White House: Rue de la Bourse 34. Tel. 513.20.83.

General Store: Chauss. de Boondael 276. Tel. 647.34.07

Markets

Bargain-hunters will have fun exploring the many flea markets in Brussels.

Place du Grand Sablon: Sat. 9am-6pm and Sun. 9am-2pm. It is the most stylish flea market in Brussels, and is also far more expensive than the usual flea markets. Old paintings, old photographs, household goods and objets d'art are sold at this market.

Place du Jeu de Balle: Every day 7am-2pm. This is considered the best flea market in Brussels, where you can find anything and everything.

Chaussée de Wavre: The first Sunday of every month. If you happen to be in Brussels on the first Sunday of the month, this market is the place to find real bargains.

The Sunday Arab Market: This can also be considered as a flea market. It is spread out around the Midi Railway Station. Here you can find exotic vegetables, roast chickens, hardware and just about anything else.

Other **flea markets** can be found at:

Place de la Resistance: Anderlecht, Saturdays 7am-1pm.

Place Saint Denis: Forest, Saturday and Sunday 9am-1pm (also second Monday of October 9am-6pm).

Rue du Collage: Ixelles, Fri.-Sat. 9am-8pm and Sun. 9am-3pm.

In Brussels there are several markets which specialize in one particular kind of merchandise.

The bird market: Every Sunday 7am-2pm at the Grand Place. One of Brussels' most interesting markets.

The flower market: Every day except Monday at the Grand' Place 8am-6pm. The best in the city.

The horse market: Every Friday, 5am-noon at Place de la Duchesse de Brabant, Molenbeek.

The domestic animal market: Sunday mornings at Ropsy Chaudron.

Books and records are on sale at the following markets:

Place d'Aumale: Anderlecht, Friday 7am-1pm.

Place de la Resistance: Anderlecht, Saturday 7am-1pm.

Place Saint Denis: Forest, Saturday 9am-1pm.

Parvis de Saint Gilles: Saint Gilles, Tuesday-Sunday 6am-noon.

Place Jourdan: Etterbeek, Sunday 7am-1pm.

Place Saint Job: Uccle, Monday 8am-1pm.

Avenue Chazel: Schaerbeek, Tuesday 8am-1pm.

Paintings and engravings can be found at:

Rue d'Aumale: Anderlecht, Friday 7am-1pm.
Place des Ecoles: Bercham, Friday 3pm-7pm..
Place Reine Astrid: Jette, Sunday 6am-noon.

Important Addresses and Phone Numbers

Accidents: Tel. 100
Police: Tel. 101
Red Cross: Tel. 105
Saint-Luc Hospital: Tel. 764.11.11
Brugmann Hospital: Tel. 477.21.11
Erasme Hospital: Tel. 526.34.02
Anti-poison centre: Tel. 345.45.45
Info-aids: Tel. 646.11.75
Ambulance: Tel. 649.11.22
S.O.S. Drugs: Tel. 537.52.52
Suicide Prevention: Tel. 640.65.65
Brussels National Airport, Zaventem: Tel. 720.71.67
Brussels Nord Railway Station: Tel. 219.26.40
Brussels Midi Railway Station: Tel. 219.26.40
Brussels Central Railway Station: Tel. 218.60.50
Brussels Tourist Office (T.I.B.): Tel. 513.89.40
Belgium Office of Tourism: Tel. 504.03.90
Sabena: 35 Rue Cardinal-Mercier. Tel. 511.90.30
Wake-up service: Tel. 1318
Belsacdm: Tel. 513.89.81, 720.24.15

EMBASSIES

U.S. Embassy: Blvd. du Regent 27. Tel. 513.38.30
British Embassy: Britannia House, Rue Joseph II 28. Tel. 217.90.00
Canadian Embassy: Avenue de Tervuren 2. Tel. 735.60.40
Australian Embassy: Guimard Center, Rue Guimard 6-8. Tel. 231.05.00
New Zealand Embassy: Blvd. du Regent 47-48. Tel. 512.10.40

DE VALK

ANTWERP

Brussels is the heart of Belgium, but Antwerp provides the country's economic pulse beat . It is a major center of finance, industry and the diamond trade. Three-quarters of Belgium's millionaires live in Antwerp. It has always been a city of merchants, and since the wealthy have traditionally been patrons of the arts, it has been a cultural center as well, and has many notable buildings and important paintings.

Lying 56 miles from the North Sea, it is a thriving river port, among the five largest in the world. Of the 18 diamond exchanges in the world, four are in Antwerp. "Antwerp Cut" is a trade term synonymous with quality.

The Town Hall flies the flags of 62 countries – one for each consulate in the city. Its Cathedral, with the soaring tower, boasts three masterpieces by Peter Paul Rubens. Rubens is undoubtedly the city's favorite son – the epitome of patrician, politician and painter. Each August 15, the people dress up for their biggest bash, the Rubens Market.

Antwerp is a city of good restaurants and cozy pubs. It has its own staunchly independent brewery, which produces a shimmering coppery brew which is still served in bulbous hand-blown glasses.

The main square, the Grote Markt, is surrounded by magnificent guild houses, a legacy of the Golden Age of the 16th century. Focal point of the square is the Brabo Fountain, wherein lies the tale of the city.

History

According to popular legend, a giant named Druon Antigonus once lived in a castle on the River Scheldt where Antwerp now stands. He collected a heavy toll from every boatman who passed his castle, and if any man could not pay, the giant chopped off his hand and threw it into the river.

In the Plantin-Moretus Museum, which contains a fascinating display on the history of printing

One fine day, a hero came along, a Roman legionnaire named Silvius Brabo, who killed the giant, cut off the giant's hand (and his head) and threw it into the river. That is how the city got its name: *hand-werpen* meaning "throwing the hand".

The city's name more probably comes from the old Flemish *Aen de Werpen*, "promontory in the river" – but this isn't nearly so romantic, and where would the city be without the Antwerp Hand, which appears on everything from coats of arms to chocolates – the symbol for "Made in Antwerp".

A scene from Antwerp's history, exhibited in the Stadhuis

Antwerp was first settled in the second century in the Gallo-Roman period, and Salian Franks settled here in the fourth and fifth centuries. A fortified "castellum" was built in the seventh century, but it was destroyed in the ninth century by Norsemen.

In the 11th century Antwerp was held by counts of Ardennes and Bouillon, including Godfrey de Bouillon who led the First Crusade. In the 13th century Antwerp passed to the dukes of Brabant, and the marriage of John II of Brabant to Margaret, daughter of Edward I, led to an alliance with England.

Antwerp flourished as the main mercantile center for English wool at the end of the 13th and beginning of the 14th century. Because of its prosperity and strategic importance as a North Sea port for Western and Central Europe, the city was coveted, fought over and

occupied many times. In 1357 it became part of Flanders when Brabant was invaded, and later it passed to Burgundy.

English, German and Italian merchants settled in the city, and Venetian ships brought trade to the harbor. Antwerp grew in importance in the 15th century, and the Antwerp Guild of St. Luke was founded in 1454 by Philip the Good, to encourage the development of the Flemish school of painters.

Prosperity increased when the rival port at Bruges silted up.

Statues depicting Antwerp's road to prosperity

The city reached a peak in the 16th century, and was Europe's chief commercial center. At this time, Paris and Antwerp were the largest European cities, far bigger than London. Antwerp became the major port for the Netherlands, and many foreign businesses were established. Industries included sugar refineries, soap works, diamond cutting, breweries, textile factories and book printing.

This golden age of prosperity and artistic achievement was disrupted by the reign of Philip II and the rule of the Spanish. Religious dissension led to the pillaging of the Cathedral in 1566, and in 1576 the Spanish sacked Antwerp. Attempts were made to Catholicize the population. Antwerp joined the Protestant rebellion led by William of Orange, who was trying to oust Philip II of Spain from the Netherlands. In 1577, while William of Orange was in Flanders, Antwerp asserted its independence from Spain and forbade the practice of Catholicism. In 1580, Parma led a campaign of reconquest for Spain, and in 1585, after a year long siege, Antwerp capitulated and the city once again belonged to Philip II. For a short time in the early 17th century, art and literature flourished again. Famous painters of the time included Rubens, David Teniers (the Elder and the Younger) and Jacob Jordaens.

Pressure from the United Provinces forced Spain to close the Scheldt in 1648. Trade dried up, the population dwindled, and Antwerp was ruined as an international center, but still had some regional importance. The city reached its lowest point at the end of the 18th century when it was in the hands of the French. (To this day there is bitterness about the French occupation, and it is advisable not to speak French in Antwerp.) When the French conquered the country in 1792, they looted Antwerp's art treasures, conscripted the men, and the city was ordered to pay France two million gold francs, and had to melt down precious metals from church treasuries to pay the debt.

In the spirit of the French Revolution, public worship was abolished, and priests were forced to take an "Oath of Hate" against the pope, kings and "people of blue blood". Those who refused were imprisoned in France, but some took the oath in order to protect their parishes. Consequently, some churches in Antwerp preserved their wealth while others lost their treasures to the French.

Antwerp was visited by Napoleon on several occasions.

Grote Markt, Antwerp's main commercial area, on a quiet morning

Antwerp's impressive Hôtel de Ville by night

Recognizing the city's strategic importance, he reopened the Scheldt, and constructed docks and a naval harbor, which initiated the revival of the city. The docks built in 1811 are still in use today.

Napoleon was defeated in the Waterloo campaign in 1815, and Antwerp became part of the United Kingdom of the Netherlands under William I. There was great opposition to the Dutch domination, and the Belgian revolution broke out in 1830. Dutch forces in Antwerp were forced to surrender in 1832 to French troops assisting King Leopold I of Belgium.

In 1843 a railway was built connecting Cologne and Antwerp. In 1862 Antwerp bought back from Holland the right to levy dues on Scheldt shipping, and the city began its period of modern expansion.

In the First World War, the government of Belgium was transferred from Brussels to Antwerp in 1914, but the city was besieged by the Germans. Winston Churchill, First Lord of the Admiralty at the time, arrived with Royal Marines and Royal Navy reinforcements, but the German army pushed even closer. The Belgian Government sailed for Ostende, and many British troops were taken prisoner.

During the Second World War, Antwerp was abandoned early, but near the end of the war, after it had been retaken by the Allies, it was attacked by the Germans.

Antwerp has recovered and expanded greatly, and today is one of Europe's busiest ports, and a major center of finance, industry, and the diamond industry.

How to Get There

BY AIR

The airport at Deurne is 4 miles from the city center. It has direct connections with Paris, Amsterdam, London, Cologne and Frankfurt and is served by 21 airlines.

Bus No. 16 connects the airport and the Central Railway Station, running every 10 minutes from about 5am to 11pm. A regular *Sabena* bus connects it with the Brussels Airport. There are no domestic flights.

The statue of Jan Olieslagers, a pioneer of flying, stands in front of the airfield.

BY TRAIN

The **Centraal Station** is at the top of the Keyserlei, one of Antwerp's main streets, and is just in front of the zoo. During the day, there are three trains per hour to Brussels Midi. During the rush hour, trains leave every five minutes. The journey takes about 30 minutes.

There are three trains per day to Paris, leaving from Berchem International Station. Trains connect the Centraal Station with Berchem every five minutes, and during rush hour every two minutes.

For information at the Centraal Station, call Tel. 204.20.40 Mon.-Sat. 8am-10pm, Sun. and holidays 9am-5pm. The Berchem telephone number is 239.74.11.

BY BUS

The regional bus station is at **Franklin Rooseveltplaats**. Buses offer frequent connections within the area. Antwerp is served several times a week by *Europabus* via a direct connection with Dusseldorf, Germany. The *Europabus* line and its affiliates have a network stretching from Scandinavia to Spain and Turkey.

BY CAR

Antwerp is served directly by the A1 from Brussels; the A14

Antwerp's Centraal Station, a tourist attraction in itself

from Ghent and from Lille in France; the E313 from Liege; the E34 from Eindhoven (Holland) and Essen in Germany. Motorway information service: Toeristische Federatie Provincie, Karal Oomsstraat 11, Tel. 216.28.10, fax 237.83.65.

Public Transportation

Antwerp has a network of city buses and an underground streetcar (premetro) system. Maps are available free of charge in the underground stations **Centraal (Diamant), Opera** and **Groenplaats**.

A single ticket costs 30 francs, but an eight-ride ticket is only 144 francs. Tourist tickets for unlimited rides cost 85 francs for one day and 140 francs for two days.

Most of the west bank of the Scheldt is industrial and suburban. Four public **tunnels** connect the two parts of the city, two for pedestrians and bicycle traffic and two – the new Kennedy Tunnel and the Waasland Tunnel (the locals call it the "rabbit burrow") for vehicles.

The broad interior of Antwerp's Centraal Station

Public transportation in the Steenplein

A fifth and sixth tunnel are being built for streetcars. In addition, there are many industrial tunnels in the port area.

CAR RENTAL

Car rental firms have all sorts of vehicles, from minibuses to prestige cars. The following are a few of the major car rental firms in Antwerp:

Avis: Plantin Moretuslei 62. Tel 218.94.96.
Autorent: Simonsstraat 42-46. Tel. 232.60.50.
Budget: Frankrijklei 70. Tel. 232.35.00.

Hertz: Mechelsesteenweg 43. Tel 233.29.92.

Time limits vary on parking meters in town; you need five-franc coins for the meters. The parking garages are well marked, although parking on the street is not so much a problem as in Brussels.

The *Royal Touring Club* of Belgium has an office in Antwerp at Quellinstraat 9, Tel. 232.44.31. The *Royal Automobile Club* of Belgium is at Appelmansstraat 25, Tel. 235.22.22. Breakdown service is available from *Wacht op de Weg*, Tel. 252.62.70, and *Touring Secours*, Tel. 353.88.88. (For driving laws, see "Brussels – How to get there".)

TAXIS

Taxis are a little less expensive than in Brussels, although night supplements are charged. The tip is included in the fare, but you may round up the amount: *Antwerp Tax*, Karel Oomsstraat 14, Tel. 238.38.38; *A.T.M.*, Steenborgerweert 20, Tel. 216.01.60; *Metropole*, Nassaustraat 21, Tel 231.31.31; *Star Taxi*, Pourbusstraat 23, Tel. 216.16.16.

Accommodation

Hotel facilities and services cover the full range of comfort and price.

The following are Antwerp's recommended hotels:

FIRST-CLASS HOTELS

Alfa De Keyser: De Keyserlei 66-70. Tel. 234.01.35, fax 232.39.70. 117 rooms.

Plaza Hotel: Charlottalei 43. Tel. 218.92.40, fax 218.88.23. 80 rooms.

Alfa Empire: Appelmansstraat 31. Tel. 231.47.55, fax 233.40.60. 70 rooms.

Alfa Theater: Arenbergstraat 30. Tel. 231.17.20, fax 233.88.58. 127 rooms.
Crest Hotel: Gerard Legrellelaan 10. Tel. 237.29.00.

Pullman Park Hotel: Desguinlei 94. Tel. 216.48.00, fax 216.47.12. rooms.

Switel: Copernicuslaan 2. Tel. 231.67.80, fax 233.02.90. 310 rooms.

Quality Inn: Luitenant Lippenslaan 66. Tel. 235.91.91.

Waldorf: Belgielei 36. Tel. 230.99.50.

Firean: Karel Oomsstraat 6. Tel. 237.02.60, fax 238.11.68.

Novotel: Luithagen-haven 6. Tel. 542.03.20, fax 541.70.93.

COMFORTABLE HOTELS

Alfa Congress: Plantin Moretuslei 136. Tel. 235.30.00, fax. 235.52.31.

Colombus: Frankrijklei 4. Tel. 233.03.90. fax 226.09.46.

MODERATE HOTELS

Antwerp Tower Hotel: Van Ertbornstraat 10. Tel. 234.01.20, fax 233.39.43. No restaurant.

Euro-Studio's: St. Jacobsmarkt 91-93. Tel. 233.00.75, fax 226.08.13.

The **Flemish Youth Hostels Association** is at Van Stralenstraat 40. Tel. 232.72.18. fax. 231.81.26; the **New International Youth Hostel** is at Provinciestraat 256. Tel. 218.94.30. fax. 281.09.35; the **International Youth Student Hostel** is at Boomevang, Volksstraat 49. Tel. 238.47.82.

SUBURBAN HOTELS

Kasteel van Brasschaat: Miksebaan 40, Brasschaat. Tel. 651.85.37. The hotel is an aging manor house set in a lovely, quiet park. About 6 miles from the city center.

Pendennis Castle: Augusijnslei 52, Brasschat. Tel. 651.01.72.

Scheldtboord: Scheldtstraat 151, Hemiksem. Tel. 877.14.14, fax. 877.12.10. About 8 miles from the city center.

Hostellerie Goreninghe: Kontichsesteenweg 78, Aartse-

laar, Tel. 457.95.86. About 6 miles from the city center.

General Information

Tourist Services

The City Tourist Office (VVV) is at Grote Markt 15. Tel. 232.01.03. fax. 231.19.37. Open Mon.-Sat. 9am-6pm; Sun. 9am-5pm. Closed on Christmas and New Year's Day.

There is also a branch opposite the Centraal Station on Koningin Astridplein. Tel. 233.05.70. Open daily 8:30am-8pm, Sat. 9am-7pm, and Sun. 9am-5pm, closed on Christmas and New Year's Day.

The City Tourist Office has a room booking service, and multi-lingual guides can be hired there from the City Guides' Exchange. Among them, the guides speak almost a dozen languages, and more than half of them speak English.

The *Provincial Tourist Office* at Karel Olmsstraat 11,.Tel. 216.28.10, fax. 237.83.65. and the *Flemish Tourist Office* (Vlaamse Toeristenbond) at St. Jacobsmarkt 45, Tel. 234.34.34, can provide information about the surrounding region.

Nature guides for the surroundings are available from the *Society of Environmental Education*, Ommeganckstraat 26, Tel. 231.84.81. Assistance with trade information and congresses and conventions is available from the *Chamber of Commerce*, Markgravestraat 12, Tel. 232.22.19, or from *Antwerp Congress City*,

Desguinlei 102, Box 12, Tel. 237.06.98.

Information about fairs is available from the *National Building Center*, Jan Van Rijswijcklaan 191, Tel. 237.28.90 or the *Sports Palace*, Schijnpoortweg 13, Tel. 324.25.75.

Antwerp is an important medical research center, and its Congress City is especially popular for medical congresses.

The **European Study and Information Center** is in the Exchange, Twaalfmaandenstraat, Tel. 231.22.66.

Keeping in Touch

Postal, telephone and telegraph service is standard. The Antwerp telephone prefix is 03 throughout Belgium (see "Brussels – Keeping in Touch"). In Antwerp, the main telephone office is at Jezusstraat 1, Tel. 232.58.10. It is open every day 8am-8pm. A branch at the Centraal Railway Station is open weekdays 9am-5pm.

The telephone book has an English index. The yellow pages are called the *Gouden Gids*.

Post offices are open weekdays 9am-5pm. The main post office at Groenplaats 43 (Tel. 231.53.70) is open until 6pm. On Saturday, the post office at Elststraat 4, Hoboken district, is open 9am-noon.

Business Hours

Office hours are generally 8:30am-5pm.

Shops are open 9am-6pm and many stay open as late as 9pm on Friday. Small shops may close for lunch and stay open later. Some shops open on Sunday from Christmas to New Year.

As is the custom throughout Europe, smaller shops and restaurants close for one to six weeks in summer.

Banking hours are 9am-4pm. Banks close on Sat., Sun. and holidays. Many banks do not close for lunch and a few are open Saturday morning. The exchange offices at the Centraal Station and at Grote Markt are open 9am-10pm and Saturday and Sunday. The American Express office is Frankrijklei 21, Tel. 232.59.20.

All **museums** close Monday. Municipal museums are also closed on January 1st and 2nd, May 1st and 12th, November 1st and 2nd, December 25th and 26th.

Tipping

Tipping is not a habit in Antwerp as it is in Brussels. Cinema ushers are not tipped. Restaurant bills are rounded up slightly. Never tip for information and do not tip a city guide, as he may feel insulted.

Medical Services

Many doctors and pharmacists speak English. A list of those on night and weekend duty (they rotate) is published in the weekend editions of the local newspapers and is available at the tourist office. Your hotel can help you, too.

Hospitals with 24-hour service:

St. Elisabeth Hospital: Lange Gasthuisstraat 45. Tel. 234.41.11.

Stuivenberg General Hospital: Lange Beeldekensstraat 267. Tel. 217.71.11.

Middelheim General Hospital: Lindedreef 1. Tel. 323.045.30.

Children's Hospital of Antwerp: Albert Grisarstraat 17. Tel. 230.58.80.

The Belgian Red Cross: Near the University Hospital at Wilrijkstraat 8, Edegem. Tel. 280.31.11.

ANTWERP – AREA BY AREA

The Shape of the City

Antwerp was established on the right bank of the River Scheldt (Schelde in Flemish), and the left bank (*linkeroever*) is a modern addition. The river is the city's lifeblood. "We thank God for the River Scheldt, and we thank the River Scheldt for everything else", is a local adage.

The **Central City**, enclosed in a crescent of large avenues named for the Allies of World War I – Italy, France, Great Britain and the United States of America – was built where the 16th-century Spanish fortifications had stood.

From the rim of the crescent, the broad expanse of the Meir leads to the tangle of streets that is the **Old Town**.

State entries were made (and uprisings staged) in **the Meir**, which means "marsh". Rubens designed eleven triumphal arches to adorn it for the arrival of the new Spanish governor in 1635. It is now a street of fashionable shops and department stores.

Many of Antwerp's streets and squares are named for painters, sculptors, architects and writers. This is not surprising, because in the 16th century, artists outnumbered butchers and bakers. It may also be the only city with a street named after the madame of

Antwerp's Centraal Station – an interesting structure dating from the 19th century

a brothel: Huikstraat, named for Joan van Huik.

Atop De Spieghel (the "Mirror" guild house)

Streets and squares were also named for the products made or sold there: Lijnwaadmarkt (Linen Market), Wolstraat (Wool Street), Varkensmarkt (Pig Market). Street names can give a clue as to where the waterways led until the last century. Streets ending in *rui* were once canals (for example *Kaasrui* means "Cheese Canal"). *Kaai* means quay and *vliet* moat.

When the French occupied the city, they translated all the street names, changing Jezusstraat to Street of the Imposter. Venijsstraat was called Venus, Meijstraat became Rue de Mai: both had been named after rich families, particular targets of the revolutionary French. However, when Antwerp regained its independence the street names were put back into Flemish. In the process it made the error of translating Mai to Mei, so that the street still bears the name of the month instead of the family.

The city tourist office has simplified the exploration of the Old Town by marking walking routes among the jumble of streets. Brochures translated into English describe the Rubens walk as well as two historic walks.

Beyond the crescent is the **Centraal Station**, a 19th-century building undergoing renovation, reached by the Keyserlei. This broad street is an extension of the Meir, and has a proliferation of movie houses, change offices and restaurants. The **Zoo**, one of the best in Europe, as fascinating for its architecture as for its animals, lies to one side of the station (see "Other Sites"). **Pelikaanstraat** is on the other side. This unassuming little street is actually the second richest in the world (after New York's Wall Street), because it is the center of the city's diamond trade.

The triangular **City Park**, one of 80 parks, is not far from the Station. The business districts around the station fan out into the Greater Antwerp area, which comprises villages which were incorporated into the city and which still retain their names: Berendrecht, Zandvliet, Berchem, Borgerhout, Deurne, Ekeren, Hoboken, Merksem and Wilrijk.

Marking the outer limits of the city is a series of forts built in 1859. Some are still used by the military, but most have been turned into recreation areas. At Lillo-Fort, there is a **yacht harbor**, at Fort V, a **Tram Museum** and at Fort VI, a **sports field**. (Lillo Harbor Center, Scheldelaan 700, Tel. 568.14.80, fax 568.18.14).

From the Old Town, the port stretches along the river northward, a giant industrial complex which has swallowed up most of the villages in its path. The tourist office provides a brochure for touring the port by car and the Flandria boating company has port cruises leaving from Kai 13, near the London Bridge.

The Flavor of Old Antwerp – Around Grote Markt and the Cathedral

One's first stop in Antwerp, the place to get one's bearings, should be the Grote Markt, the central market place. In Frankish tradition, it is roughly triangular. There are many sites within walking distance of the Grote Markt.

The **Stadhuis** (Town Hall) stands in solitary splendor on the river side of the Market. Grote Markt 1. Tel. 220.82.11. Open Mon. Tues. Wed. Fri. 9am-3pm, Sat. 12pm-4pm. Closed Sundays and public holidays. The building was built during the years 1561-1565 by a group of local architects, headed by Cornelis Floris, as an expression of the Renaissance spirit of Antwerp's Golden Age.

Scarcely a decade later, it was damaged during the "Spanish Fury". The Spanish troops had not been paid for several months; they grew restless and were sent into the city to "pay themselves". In the looting of November 4, 1576, most of the houses on the Grote Markt were burnt, including the Town Hall.

The Town Hall was restored in a short space

Antwerp's Town Hall, the Stadhuis

of time and has suffered little from the changes in succeeding architectural styles. Many of the artworks acquired in the 17th and 18th centuries were destroyed or stolen during the French occupation. The building was redecorated in its present form in the 19th century.

It contains paintings by a number of important artists. One picture shows a Negro being accepted as a free citizen of Antwerp, with the inscription "In the City of Antwerp,

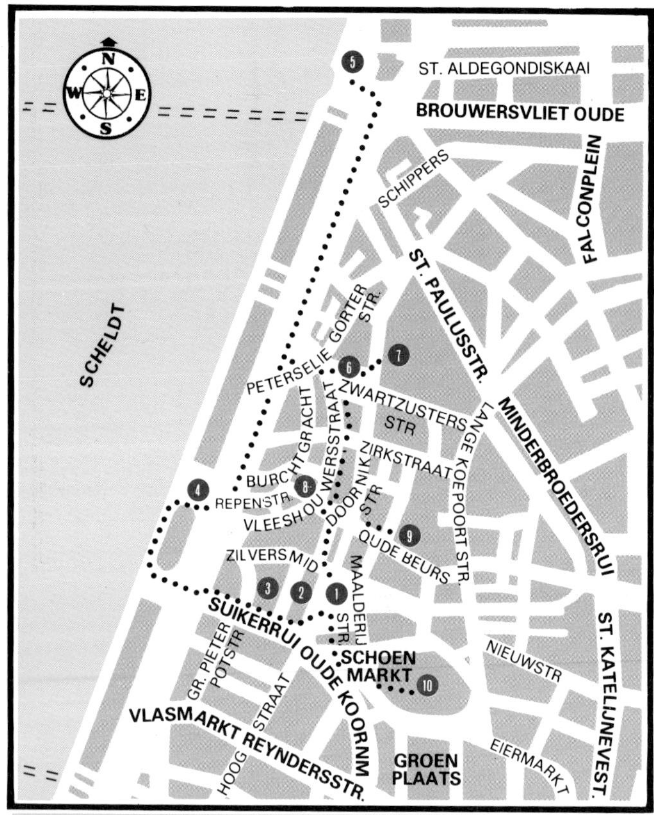

AROUND GROTE MARKT AND THE CATHEDRAL

1. Grote Markt
2. Stadhuis (Town Hall)
3. Folklore Museum
4. Steen
5. Pilot's Station
6. Vee Markt
7. St. Paul's Church
8. Vleeshuis
9. De Spieghel
10. The Cathedral

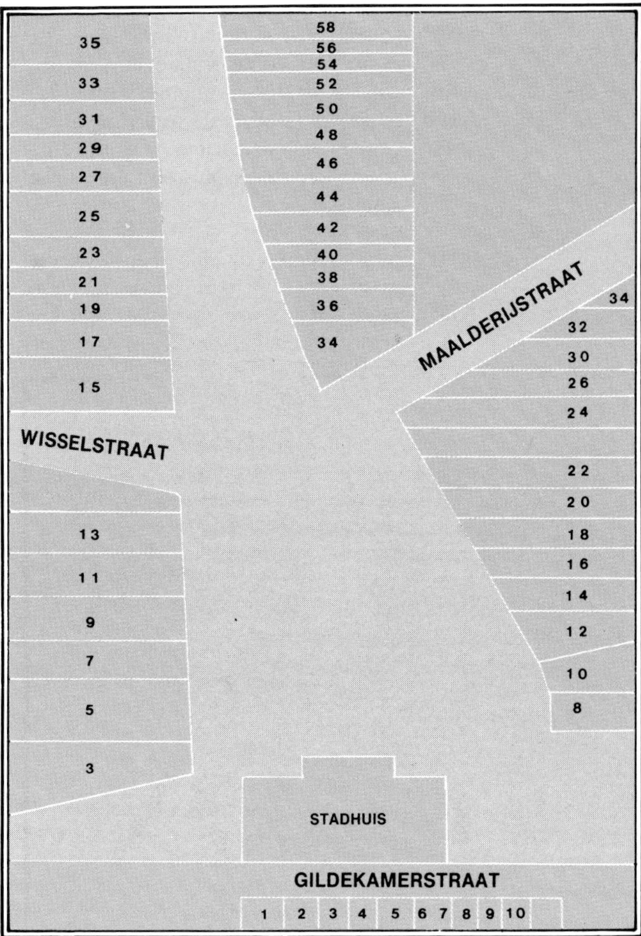

GROTE MARKT

all people are free and there are no slaves". A number of Negroes lived in the city in the 16th century, and all worked as painters' models.

Guided tours of the building include the Leys Room, the former Lords' Chamber, decorated with historical paintings representing the main privileges of the city; the small Leys Room, which was formerly a staircase; the Marriage Chamber, with paintings of marriage scenes from several

Impressive 19th century interior decor in the Stadhuis

historical periods; the Lord Mayor's Room, with a huge chimney and a table made from the Tree of Liberty which once stood on the market place.

On the front of the building, the coat of arms of Philip II of Spain (ruler of the Netherlands) forms the central carving. To the right is the coat of arms of the Margravate of Antwerp and to the left, that of the duchy of Brabant. Between them stand the allegorical figures of Justice (without blindfold) and Wisdom.

The Virgin Mary, the city's patron, stands in the niche above. The eagle on top faces Aachen, the centre of the rule of Charlemagne.

The other two sides of the Grote Markt are lined with guild houses, many topped with statues of the patron saint with the trade or symbol. The guilds were organizations of skilled craftsmen. As they became rich and powerful, the guilds would build a house for their gatherings, then build their own altar in the Cathedral. Next they would build a chapel in town (three or four remain), and finally, a "retirement home" for members, of which a few remain, too.

Stained glass at the Stadhuis

Most of the façades on the market place are reconstructions, although some are original, for example No. 38, the **Drapers' House** (17th century), No. 40, the **Carpenters' House** and the 18th-century house on the corner at No. 24.

Facing the Town Hall, the houses to the right have odd numbers and those to the left, even. Beginning at Braderijstraat, No. 3 is **De Witte Engel** (White Angel); No. 5 is **De Gulden Mouw** (Golden Sleeve, the coopers' guild house) topped by a statue of

St. Matthias; No. 7 is **Hais Spaengien** (Spanish House, the artists' guild); No. 9 is **De Spieghel** (the Mirror, the archers' guild) with a statue of St. Sebastian; No. 11 is **Den Zwarte Arend** (Black Eagle, a mercantile guild for dealers in sewing notions) topped by an image of an eagle; No. 13 is **De Pauw** or **De Vos** (Peacock or Fox, guild of medieval gunners) with a figure of a fox, and next door is **De Bonte Mantel** (Coat of Many Colors).

Across Wisselstraat are No. 15, a reconstucted brewery façade named **Den Grooten Luypaert** with a symbolic lion statue; No. 17, **Den Regenboghe** (Rainbow); No. 19, **De Meersman** (Sellers of sewing notions); No. 21 **Den Beer** (Bear); No. 23, **De Schminkel** (Fool); No. 25, **Het Wapenschild** (Coat of Arms) and No. 27, **Den Kemel** (Camel).

On the other side of the street, the houses are No. 48, **De Groote Wolvinne** (Large She-Wolf); No. 46, **De Kleine Wolvinne** (Small She-Wolf); No. 44, **De Witten Ketel** (White Kettle); No. 40, **Rodenborch** (Red Fortress, the carpenters' guild); No. 38, **De Oude Waag** or **De Gulden Balans** (Old Weigh-House or Golden Scales, wool merchants' guild; No. 36 **De Keyser** (Emperor); No. 34, **Gulden Valk** (Golden Falcon) topped by a falcon.

The original surviving façade of the Carpenters' house

Grote Markt's surrounding streets are lined with small cafés

Across Maalderijstraat is No. 24, **Grote Mond Toe** (Shut Your Big Mouth, referring to the notion that Antwerpians are prone to chatter) in rococo style; **Het Gulden Schaap** (Golden Sheep); No. 22, **De Fortune Het Avontuur** (Fortune, Adventure); No. 20, **De Gulden Wereld** (Golden World); No. 18, **Het Gulden Paard** (Golden Horse); No. 16, **Den Gulden Beer** (Golden Bear); No. 10 **De Zon** (Sun).

Before you leave the market place, take a look at the **Brabo Fountain**, the main feature of the Grote Markt. It was sculpted in 1887 by Jef Lambeaux. A victorious Brabo is flinging the hand of the giant Antigonus into the river Scheldt (See "Antwerp – History").

You may wish to stop for a beer at one of the many cafés and restaurants that line the square. In summer, horse-drawn carriages clatter up the cobbled street promptly at noon, ready to give tourists a ride through the Old Town.

Just behind the Town Hall, on Gildekamersstraat, is the city's Tourist Information Office. (There is also an information booth in front of the Centraal Station).

The Folklore Museum (Volkskundemuseum) is at Gildekamersstraat 2-6. Tel. 220.86.53, ext. 383. Open daily 10am-5pm, closed Mondays. Closed on 1-2 Jan., 1 May, Ascension Day, 1-2 Nov and 25-26 Dec. The museum is housed in five restored guild houses.

The museum was established in

1907, when the city of Antwerp acquired the collection of Max Eslkamp, who was a poet and wood engraver. The museum surveys Flemish life as expressed in pageants and processions, popular devotion, art, customs, social life and recreation.

There is also a collection of objects pertaining to popular medicine and magic, plus a collection of some 5000 popular prints and more than 150 puppets. There are also exhibits of Gallo-Roman pottery, old pharmaceutical equipment, musical instruments, games, playing cards, costumes and jewelry.

The Suikerrui (Sugar Canal) leads down from Grotemarkt to the **Steenplein**, the river front where the city began. There is a statue of the Goddess Minerva here. Face away from the river for an excellent view of the Cathedral spire. Flandria boats dock here for river cruises. There are daily 50 minute river cruises leaving from the Steenplein from April to the end of September. A longer cruise of an hour and a quarter operates less frequently.

A view of Our Lady's Cathedral from the Steenplein

To the north of the Steenplein is the **Steen** itself. The gatehouse and front section are remnants of the ancient Antwerp castle. (Shaepvaartmuseum), was installed in Steen castle and opened to the public in 1952. The museum also includes some of the adjoining quays along the river. (Steenplein 1, Tel. 232.08.50. Open daily 10am-5pm.) Excavations in and around the buildings have brought to light traces of settlement from Gallo-Roman times. The castle was restored in 1520 by order of Emperor Charles V, and for some time served as a prison. In 1862 an archeological museum opened in the Steen, and in 1948 Antwerp's museums were reorganised and the **National Maritime Museum** (Museum open Tues.-Sun. 10am-5pm. Closed Mon. Jan. 1-2, May 1, Nov.1-2, Dec. 25-26. Tel. 232.08.50)

The museum contains beautiful models of steam and sailing ships, navigation instruments, charts, and an explanation of the history of boat building. In the Council Chamber No. 12 you will find paintings by Bonaventure and Bonnecroy which depict life in old Antwerp and its waterfront. A couple of old wooden cranes have been set up beside the museum, and berthed alongside, in one of the ornate boat sheds, is the barge **Laurande**, which gives you an idea of how people lived on the river. At berth No. 22 there are boats, steam engines, winches, port equipment, cranes and vehicles.

In front of the Steen is the larger-than-life **Lange Wapper statue**, a legendary Antwerp character who frightened folk – especially those who had had a drink too many – by being able to grow at will and peer into windows. Along the North Promenade you can get a good view of the river, though most of the shipping activity has moved out of sight to the new port.

The Steen – remnants of an ancient castle

At St. Paul's Church

You can continue northward to the neo-Gothic **Loodswezengebouw** (pilot's station). Because the Scheldt is so difficult to navigate, specially trained pilots must guide ships on the river. There is another statue of Brabo here, and a monument to those killed at sea in the two World Wars. Across the river is a yacht harbor. If you skip the promenade, return to town by Peterselie, which leads to the **Vee Markt** (Cattle Market).

At the corner of Zwartaustersstraat (Paulusstraat st. 20-22) is the entrance to **St. Paul's Church**, the richest in Antwerp. Open May-Sept. 2-5pm; Oct.-April 9am-noon. Closed Sunday and Monday. Guided visits on request. Tel. 232.32.67). The church is mainly 16th century late Gothic, with a 17th century baroque tower built for the Dominicans. The Gothic exterior gives no hint of the riotous baroque within. The interior is known for its panelling, wood carving and paintings. Over the south transept altar is the *Disputation on the Blood Sacrament* by Rubens, painted soon after his return from Italy. Another painting, *The Scourging* (1617), by Rubens hangs at the east end on the north aisle. The church also has works by Jordaens and Van Dyck. A fire in 1968 damaged much of the church, but fortunately paintings by Rubens, Van Dyck, Jordaens and Teniers were saved. There is also a copy of Mt. Calvery in Jerusalem, where Jesus was buried.

Incidentally, the support of art by business is a continuing tradition in Antwerp. The Monsanto Company restored the entrance to St. Paul's, and other firms are sponsoring other restoration projects.

Another Gothic jewel – so grand that it might be mistaken for a church – is the butchers' guild house, the **Vleeshuis**. (From the Vee Markt walk down Vleeshouw-

Sculptures at St. Paul's Church garden

ersstraat). Appropriately enough, its red brick is alternated with layers of "fat" white sandstone.

The butchers were one of the richest and most powerful of all the guilds in Antwerp, and they snubbed the Grote Markt to build here instead. The ground floor had space for 62 stalls where they could sell meat. Upstairs were the meeting rooms and a chapel.

The house is now a museum. (Vleeshouwersstraat 38-40. Tel. 233.64.04. Open daily except Monday 10am-5pm. Closed 1-2 Jan., 1 May, Ascension Day, 1-2 Nov. and 25-26 Dec.) It contains applied arts, archeology and local history – a fascinating hodgepodge of everything from weather vanes to clerical robes. The museum has exhibits on carving, the manufacturing of harpsichords, ceramics, glassware, cabinet and jewelry making.

At the top of a steep and narrow circular staircase is a display of weapons, which are also depicted in a series of period paintings. The large collection of musical instruments includes examples of harpsichords made by a famous manufacturer from Antwerp called Ruckers. Ruckers was for harpsicords what Stradivarius was for violins, his workshop made Antwerp the center of harpsichord manufacture in the 17th century.

Looking a little out of place at one end of the music room is the Vleeshuis Mummy, lying in an ornate sarcophagus. The inscription describes it as the body of Nes-Chonsoe, one of Amon-Re's singers, dating from about 945 BC. Whether it was a gift, or stolen, from Egypt, we don't know. The *Averbode Retable* (1514) by Jacob van Cothem depicts Christ's Entombment. There is also an interesting wall tile picture (1547) depicting Saul's conversion to Paul.

Downstairs in the cellar, is a fascinating salvage yard of statues and gravestones. The most distinctive aspect of the Vleeshuis is the building itself, with arched ceilings, dark wood and winding stone stairs.

Across the street, at Repenstraat 3, is the **Poesje** puppet theater where shows can be arranged for groups only, in either clean or spicy Antwerp dialect.

Turn down Oude Beurs for a look at **De Spieghel** (the Mirror) at No. 16. It takes its name from the relief of a woman admiring herself in a mirror while her children gaze adoringly at her. Sir Thomas Moore stayed here in 1515 when he was writing *Utopia*.

Backtrack to Braderijstraat for a look at the Brabant late Gothic façades of Nos. 12, 14 and 16. Just around the corner is the Grote Markt.

Much of this area has been rebuilt: in 16th-century style, in broken rows with sharp roofs.

Our Lady's Cathedral

THE CATHEDRAL – AN UNFINISHED MASTERPIECE

From the Grote Markt, the small Maalderijstraat leads to the Handschoenmarkt, named for the glove merchants.

Towering above this small square is the **Our Lady's Cathedral**, the largest Gothic church in Belgium, with typically Brabant details and a spire 403 feet tall. (Tel. 231.30.33. Open Mon.-Fri. 10am-5pm, Sat. and eve of church holidays 10am-3pm, Sun. 1pm-4pm. Tel. 231.30.33).

Before going into the Cathedral, stop at the little well at the edge of the square. Here Brabo appears again, in uniform, in wrought iron.

The well was made by a smith by the name of Quinten Metsys, who fell in love with an artist's daughter. Her father felt that a smith was not good enough for her, so Metsys took up painting and founded an Antwerp school of art. The text in the stone of the well says, "Love made a painter of a blacksmith". Metsys' burial plaque is to the left of the Cathedral entrance.

It is pleasant to sit nearby in one of the outdoor cafés for carillon concerts at noon, and on Monday evenings at 9pm between June 15 and September 30.

To the right of the main entrance to the Cathedral is a group of figures by Jef Lambeaux showing the master builder Appelmans with the plan of the tower on his knee, speaking to his masons. Since the Cathedral took 170 years (1352-1521) to build, (and even then the second tower was never completed), there were other master builders besides Appelmans. In 1794 many of the art treasures were seized by the French, but some were later retrieved when the Cathedral reopened in 1802.

Rubens' *Elevation of the*

Cross, *The Descent from the Cross* and *the Assumption of the Virgin Mary* hang here. In the Cathedral you can also see *The Last Supper* by Otto Venius, *Marriage at Cana* by Martin de Vos and other treasures. Be sure to go during visiting hours, or you will not be admitted.

From the Cathedral to the Printing Museum

Metro: Meir
Tram: 8, 10
Bus: 9

The streets around the Cathedral are filled with lace, chocolate, book and antique shops, and many wonderful old Antwerp cafés.

The café at Oude Koornmarkt 48 was the headquarters of the Resistance during World War II. Notice the step-gabled houses along this street. No. 26, **De Cluyse,** was given to the German Hanse (a merchants' league) by the city council in the 15th century. At No. 16, you can walk through the intimate Vlaaikensgang to Pelgrimstraat, and from there to Reyndersstraat.

At Reyndersstraat 25 you will find *De Vagant*. It is one of the city's typical beer-cafés, but with a difference: it is also a veritable gin palace.

A two-toned cat curls up beside the bar; behind it, green bottles sparkle and thick brown ones stand on the shelves, to the strains of classical music, tall and straight as a row of soldiers.

Genever, sometimes spelled "Jenever", is the gin of the Low Countries. Visitors to the Netherlands may be familiar with *oude* (old) and *jonge* (young) genever, but *De Vagant* stocks 164 different kinds, all but two made in Belgium, and owner Ronald Ferket still hasn't tracked them all down.

He is doing research into the history of Belgian genever, and has founded a group of

A statue of Rubens, with Our Lady's Cathedral in the background

people who get together for tasting sessions, and who hope to develop a language to use in talking about genever, as the terms that are used to describe wines are not suitable to describe spirits.

Genever is an after-dinner drink for Belgians, and it is not drunk as an accompaniment to beer as the Germans drink *schnapps* with beer. Ferket explains that one can mix young genever with juice or cola, but not old genever.

If you turn left, Reyndersstraat leads to the Meir going past the Groenplaats, which was a cemetery until Napoleon turned it into a park. A **statue of Rubens** stands in the center, and concerts and chess matches are held here in summer.

De Vagant at Reyndersstraat – a beer café and gin palace

If you turn in the opposite direction down Reyndersstraat, you will come to **Jacob Jordaens' House**. (Reyndersstraat 4, Tel. 234.39.85. Open daily 10am-5pm.) Jordaens (1593-1678) followed in Rubens' footsteps, and even completed some works left unfinished by the latter. Jordaens' house, built in

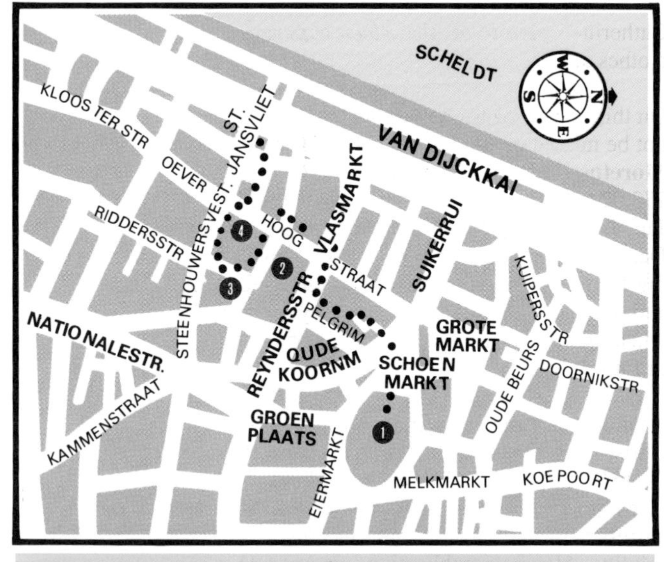

FROM THE CATHEDRAL TO THE PRINTING MUSEUM

1. The Cathedral
2. Jacob Jordaens' House
3. Vrijdagmarkt
4. Plantin–Moretus Museum

1641, reflects his wealth. He was actually born just a few steps away from here at Hoogstraat 11-13.

Continue to Hoogstraat, a street of shops selling old books and antiques. Turn left, then left again on Heilig-Geeststraat for a look at one of the oldest surviving patrician houses in Antwerp. No. 9 is called **Den Gulden Cop** (Golden Head) or **Huis Draecke** (Dragon House), and the west wing dates from the 15th century. The 16th-century polygonal tower is an example of the Antwerp "pagaddertoren" (house-tower).

The street opens out onto the **Vrijdag Markt** (Friday Market) where auctions of second-hand goods are held each Wednesday and Friday morning. This has been a tradition since 1549. The statue here is of Sainte

Catherine, patron of the *cleercoopers* – clothes sellers.

On this square stands a museum that should not be missed on any account. The **Plantin-Moretus Museum**. (Vrijdag Markt 22, Tel. 233.02.94. Open daily 10am-5pm. Closed Jan. 1-2, May 1, Ascension Day, Nov. 1-2, Dec. 25-26). It not only contains a fascinating history of printing, but the house itself and its furnishings are just as they were when the family reigned as premier printers in Europe.

Founder of the printing dynasty was Christopher Plantin, who came to Antwerp in 1549. A bookbinder by trade, he was forced to change his job due to injuries he suffered in an attack, and he took up printing. His first publication appeared in 1555.

Plantin was an interesting and powerful personality, who became Europe's premier printer. He became the printer to King Philip II of Spain, and was given the monopoly for the sale of liturgical books in Spain and the Spanish colonies. Plantin had 16 printing presses and an enormous printing shop, while the leading French printing family in

A work of art in the Plantin-Moretus Museum

The Plantin-Moretus Museum, named after Christopher Plantin, a premier printer in 16th century Europe

the 16th century (Estiennes) had only 4 presses.

Plantin moved to Vrijdagmarkt in 1576, and after his death, his son-in-law Jan Moretus took over control of the business, and after him the business was run by his son Balthasar, who was a good friend of Rubens. For 300 years the family printing tradition continued, until 1876 when Edward Moretus sold the building with its contents to the City of Antwerp. The museum includes family portraits (many by Rubens), woodblocks, copper plates, manuscripts, furniture and presses.

One major item on display is the *Biblia Regia* or *Biblia Polyglotta*. With financial help from King Philip II of Spain, and with help from King Philip's chaplain Arias Montanus, the Biblia Regia was produced in Latin, Greek, Hebrew, Syriac and Aramaic. The publication included grammatical and other appendices, and took from 1568-1572 to complete.

The museum collection has some beautiful 15th century miniatures, rare 16th century tapestries, ancient and rare manuscripts, a selection of drawings and title pages by masters who worked for the Plantin firm, such as Martin de Vos, Adam van Noort, Van der Horst and P. de Joode. In room 19 there are also sketches and engravings by Rubens, who did some illustrations for Plantin.

Room No. 23, the Geographical Room, includes maps and atlases from the 16th to 18th centuries. Especially interesting is a map of Antwerp from 1565. In Room No. 24 you can see one of the most interesting exhibits – one of the 13 known copies of the

36 line Gutenberg Bible, which were printed for Philip II.

Adjoining is the **City Print Room** (Vrijdagmarkt 23), a collection begun by Max Rooses, first curator of the Plantin-Moretus Museum. His original purpose was to collect the prints and drawings which had illustrated the publications of Plantin and his successors, but the work soon expanded to first cover Flemish graphic art in the 16th and 17th centuries, and then the 18th and 19th centuries. Today the collection contains almost 12,000 drawings and thousands of prints, copperplates and woodcuts.

Leave the Vrijdagmarkt by Steenhouwersvest, where stone-cutters and masons once had their shops, and return to Hoogstraat, pausing at the corner of St. Jansvliet where St. Julian's Hospital stood. It was built for pilgrims on their way to Santiago de Compostella, Spain. At the end of St. Jansvliet is the building which leads to a pedestrian tunnel under the river. Hoogstraat takes you back to the Grote Markt.

Old printing machines

A Glimpse of a Golden Age – From Grote Markt to Rubens' House

Tram: 3, 10
Bus: 9

Leave the Grote Markt opposite the Town Hall, and walk down the Kaasrui. Pause at the corner of Torfburg beside the "hangman's house". Look closely at the worn bas-relief which gives the house its name. The scaffolding really does look like gallows, but in reality it marked the house of the masons.

Antwerp had a hangman, of course, but he was never a local man. He had a price list for various forms of punishment, but couldn't earn enough to live on, so he also worked as the city dog-catcher, and collected taxes from the prostitutes.

Turn left on Lange Koepoortstraat, then turn right on Wolstraat for a look at the Spanish portals at No. 7 and No. 30. The house at No. 38 has been restored. Peek into the courtyard of No. 37. The cottages around it were built for aged members of the Furriers' Guild.

Turn right onto Hendrik Conscienceplein, named for the 19th-century author who addressed social problems of Antwerp.

The Art Gallery at Rubens' House

When he began writing in Flemish, he encouraged a revival of its use as a written language. An antiques and flea market takes place on the square on summer Saturdays.

The rich and ornate interior of the Church of St. Charles Borromeo

Towering over the square is the Jesuit-baroque **Church of St. Charles Borromeo**. (Tel. 233.24.33 Hendrik Conscienceplein 12. francs. Guided visits Wednesday 2 – 3pm. Open Mon. 10am-Tues.-Sun. 9am-noon Mon. Wed. and Fri. also 2pm-6pm, Sat. also 3pm-6:30 pm.) The church was originally dedicated to the Virgin Mary, then to St. Ignatius and then to Charles Borromeo, cardinal-archbishop of Milan, who was known for the help he gave to the poor.

The church, built from 1615-1621, was designed by the Jesuit architect Pieter Huyssens, but Rubens also contributed to the design of the façade, and did much of the interior decoration. Unfortunately much of Rubens' work was destroyed in a fire caused by lightning in 1718. The church was reconstructed the following year in Rubens' baroque style. The Lady Chapel, which survived the fire, is lined with the colored marble which was a main feature of the earlier church.

From the square, turn down St. Katelijnevest, which takes you to the Meir, passing the Exchange (at Waalfmaandenstraat) and then the Agencie Maritime International Building on the left.

The first **Exchange** (Handelsbeurs) was built at Hofstraat 15 (now the City Education Department), but the premises soon became too small. Dominic de Waghemakere designed splendid new ones, which

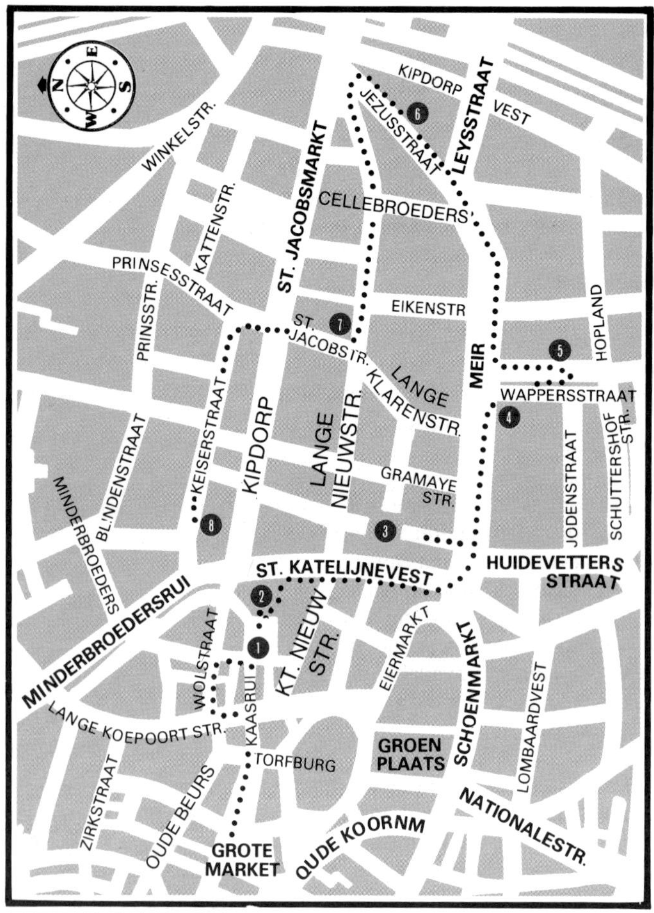

GROTE MARKT TO RUBENS' HOUSE

1. Hendrik Conscienceplein
2. Church of St. Charles Borromeo
3. Exchange
4. Royal Palace
5. Rubens' House
6. National Security Institute
7. St. Jacob's Church
8. Rockox House

opened in 1531, but they did not please the English merchants, so they built their own – the Engelse Beurs. This was rather short-lived, since the merchants fled to Hamburg during the Reign of Terror 35 years later.

The present building, actually reached from the Meir by way of the tiny Twaalf-Maandenstraat, is an 1872 reconstruction of the

1531 Exchange, which burnt down in 1858. It served as model for many other European exchanges, including Gresham's in London.

Continue along the Meir, to the corner of Wappersstraat – the former **Royal Palace** (Meir 50). It is rococo on the outside but with a starkly modern addition through the courtyard. Nowadays, it is an international cultural center.

Turn right into the Wapper, a wide promenade which was made by joining Rubens and Wappers streets, where a canal used to run in Rubens' time. **Rubens' House** is at 9-11 Wapper. (Tel. 232.47.47. Open Tues.-Sun. 10am-5pm. Closed public holidays. Admission Fee). The house is a reconstruction of the Flemish Renaissance mansion where the artist lived and worked from 1616 until his death. Visitors in his day spoke of the luxury of the furnishings. The spacious house and gardens bear the stamp of the artist. A booklet is available in English (at the ticket window) for a detailed description of the interior.

One of the statues found in the grounds of Rubens' House

Although Rubens completed his studies in Italy, he was still, to a large extent, faithful to the Flemish school of painting. Rubens gained more fame and success in his lifetime than any previous artist, and could afford a very lavish lifestyle, which explains the size and character of the house which he built for himself and his wife in 1517. His house soon became a center for the "high society" of Flanders.

The house was famous not just because of its famous owner, but also because of the rare contents, which today are found in museums and churches throughout the world.

Although the house today contains only a small part of the work of

The interior courtyard of Rubens' House

Rubens and his pupils, and although the furniture is not all original but rather antique furniture from Rubens' time, a visit to the house nevertheless helps to shed light on many aspects of the life and times of the artist.

We can start our visit in the interior courtyard with its surprising baroque structure. The portico, which separates the yard from the garden, has been immortalized in many Rubens paintings which can be seen today in the Louvre Museum in Paris. The statues of Mercury and Minerva above the portico are 20th century replacements of the original statues.

The exterior wall of the studio is decorated with sculptures and scenes taken from the Greek and Roman worlds. Philosophers and rulers are depicted alongside mythological characters.

The garden beyond the portico was redone according to one of Rubens' paintings. The pavilion has been preserved in relatively good condition and shows Rubens' feeling for Greek and Roman mythology.

In the Parlour we can see an enlargement of

a print of 1692, which gives an idea of Rubens' house at the time. This room also contains *The Presentation in the Temple* by Jacob Jordaens. We can also see *The Adoration of the Magi* by Van Noort who was one of Rubens' teachers.

In the Dining Room there is a self portrait by Rubens, probably painted in his late forties.

The Art Gallery used to house the Master's art collection and included paintings by Rubens himself and by other artists such as Van Eyck, Titian and Raphael. On the death of Rubens the collection was dispersed. Today it is once again an art gallery, and among the paintings we can see, to the right of the door, is *Christmas Night* by Van Leyden. To the right of it hangs *Landscape with Rainbow* by Lucas van Uden. Nearby is an oil sketch by Rubens, *The Adoration of the Shepherds*.

On the narrow wall to the left of the entrance to the Sculpture Gallery we can see a work by Jan Breughel: *Albert and Isabella in the Coudenberg Gardens*. In the Gallery we can see *The Art Room of Cornelius van der Geest*, by Willem Van Hacht.

Upstairs is the Large Bedroom – where Rubens died in 1640. On the wall nearest the door is a portrait of Nicholas Rockox attributed to Otto Venius, the most important of Rubens' teachers. Also worth noting is a gold medallion with a relief of King Christian IV of Denmark.

Warm up to this rich atmosphere at Rubens' House

In the Small Bedroom there is a portrait of Helene Fourment, Rubens' second wife. In the Linen Room there are two paintings by Jordaens: *Moses and his Ethiopian Wife* and *Mercury Kills Argus*. In the middle of this room is a 17th century five-door Antwerp cupboard.

The broad expanse of the Meir – a street of fashionable shops and department stores

In the Corner Bedroom is Rubens' chair, used when he was Dean of the Guild of St. Luke. The Living Room contains two portraits of Rubens' grandparents and a *View of Antwerp* by Pieter Snayers.

On the Landing we see the *Lamentation* by Jordaens and in the Pupils' Studio we can see 17th century prints of Rubens' work. In the Private Studio, which was also used as an office, there are several paintings by Rubens and others.

Return to the Meir and follow it to its end, where it branches off into Leysstraat and Jezusstraat. Settled into a niche of the corner house is a statue of **Lodewyk van Bercken**, who perfected the art of diamond polishing, thus paving the way for Antwerp's excellent reputation.

Leysstraat leads to De Keyserlei and the Central Station. Turn down Jezusstraat for a visit to the **National Security Institute**, which has an exhibition of the diamond trade. (Jezusstraat 28-30, Tel. 324.87.50. Open Wed.-Sun. 10am-5pm. Closed 1-2 Jan. and 25-26 Dec. On Sat. there are demonstrations of diamond cutting 2-5pm. Entry free.) The diamond industry is concentrated in the area around Pelikaanstraat.

The Diamond Museum explains how diamonds are found, sorted, worked, polished, and used in jewellry and industry. Photographs, tools and instruments and a slide show make for an interesting visit.

Return to the Meir Markt by way of the Lange Nieuwstraat, stopping to look into **St. Jacob's Church**. (Lange Nieuwstraat 73. Open daily except Sunday and holidays, from April 1 to Oct. 31, 2-5pm; from Nov. 1 to March 31, 9am-noon, except during services. Admission Fee. Tel. 232.10.32) Here you will find Rubens' burial chapel, among other chapels and altars of many of the leading families of Antwerp. This is another of Antwerp's rich churches, a Gothic structure filled with baroque and rococo.

The original chapel was built in 1413, and work on the present church was begun in 1491 by Herman de Waghemakere. The work was continued after his death by his sons and later by Rombout Keldermans.

Paintings include those by Otto Venius, Jordaens and Rubens (this is the church where Rubens attended Mass), and there are sculptures by Michiel Van der Voort, Colijns de Nole and H.F. Verbruggen.

The main attraction is the chapel dedicated to Rubens. This is the fourth chapel from the south in the Ambulatory. Here you will see one of the greatest works of the artist – the *Virgin, Infant and Saints*, which was painted specially for this chapel. It seems likely that the figures in the painting are actually portraits of Rubens' family. Rubens has used a self-portrait as St. George, his two wives as Martha and Mary Magdalene, his father as St. Jerome, and his son as Jesus.

Antwerp – a diamond city

We shall note just a few of the many works in the chapel. In the third chapel (from the south), dedicated to one of the many merchant families of Antwerp, is a Van Dyck painting *The Crucifixion* and a sculpture of *The Raising of the Cross*. In the fifth chapel, dedicated to St. Carolus Borromeus, is a portrait of the archbishop painted by Jacob Jordaens.

In the first chapel on the north aisle we can see *Constantine the Great Kneeling before the Cross Held by St. Helena* – the work of Wenceslas Coeberger. On the south aisle the first chapel includes the Van Dyck painting *St. George and the Dragon*.

If you still have the energy, cut over to Keizerstraat 10 by way of Prinsesstraat to admire the **Rockox House**. It is a restored 17th-century town house of burgomaster Nicholas Rockox with authentic furniture, paintings and tapestry. (Tel. 231.47.10. Open daily except Mon. 10am-5pm. Entry Free).

Other Sites

Here are a few sites in Antwerp, which are not situated close to any of our walking routes, yet are worth a visit.

Museum voor Schone Kunsten (Fine Arts)

This museum is at Leopold de Waelplaats. (Tel. 238.78.09. fax. 248.08.10. Open Tues.-Sun. 10am-5pm. Closed Jan. 1, May 1, Ascension Day, Nov. 1 and Dec. 25).

The collection is housed in a large and well lit building (1884-1890) in neoclassical style designed by J.J. Winders and F. van Dyck. The two chariots surmounting the edifice are the work of Belgian sculptor Thomas Vincotte.

It spans five centuries of painting, and is based on the private collection of Florent van Ertborn, burgomaster of Antwerp. The speciality is 15th century art, and the collection is growing.

The top floor concentrates on Flemish primitives and has works by Jan van Eyck, Rogier van der Weyden, Joachim Patinir, Quentin Metsys and others. Foreign artists, such as Simone Martini and Lucas Cranach are also exhibited. Masters of the Antwerp

The Museum voor Schone Kunsten – the Fine Arts Museum

school included are Rubens, Van Dyck and Jordaens.

The ground floor has a huge collection of modern Belgian painting by J. Ensor, H. Evenpoel, C. Permeke, R. Wouters, J. Smits and others. There are paintings and sculptures by foreign artists as well.

The Zoo and the Museum of Natural History

Koningin Astridplein 26, Tel. 231.16.40. fax. 231.00.18. Open daily 9am-5pm or 9am-6:30pm, depending on the season. Entry fee includes entrance to both the zoo and the Natural History Museum on the premises.

At the entrance to the Zoo

It is not surprising that there is a variety of exotic animals in Antwerp. The city has been an important port for centuries, and ship captains were wont to bring home anything interesting they found on their voyages. Strange creatures from the Far East, South America and Africa are recorded on the canvasses of Rubens, Brueghel and other local painters.

It was not until 1841, however, (11 years after Belgium became an independent nation), that a permanent zoo was established in Antwerp. Originally just outside a city gate, the zoo is now in the middle of town beside the Central Railway Station.

As the zoo developed, it also became the city's cultural center, with a concert hall and the **Natural History Museum** on the premises. The museum has a valuable collection of microscopes, paintings by the animal painter Karel Verlat, and a noteworthy collection of birds.

The zoo made a name for itself internationally when the **okapi** was discovered in 1901. The okapi is a hoofed animal that looks like a mixture of giraffe and antelope. It was found in the Belgian Congo (now Zaire) by Sir Harry Johnston of London. After several trials, it was successfully bred at Antwerp, and today the okapi remains the pride of the Antwerp Zoo.

Jungle-like vegetation at the Zoo

The zoo also got first claim on the Congo peafowl, another previously unknown animal which lives only in the forests of Central Africa. Among other rare and exotic creatures, the zoo includes Matschie tree kangaroos, baby rusas, hornbills, Komodo dragons, electric eels, piranhas, frogmouths and quetzals.

The zoo suffered considerably during World War II. Initially, carnivorous animals which could not be fed had to be killed. Then, when there were food shortages, animals were slaughtered to feed the people. Only the rarest and most valuable animals were saved.

Rebuilding began soon after the war, and in 1968, a lengthy Jubilee Project was undertaken to include a Dolphinarium, an Insect House and a Nocturnal House.

The architecture of the Antwerp Zoo is just as fascinating as its animals. Perhaps the best animal house is the Egyptian Temple, built in 1856 when "Egyptomania" was sweeping through Europe. A local architect, Charles Servais, designed the building in the basilica style and had it decorated with Egyptian paintings and hieroglyphics. It is now being restored, and when completed it will once again house the elephants.

In Cogels-Osylei – a chic neighborhood in Antwerp's heart

The zoo is innovative in its displays, too. The aquarium has tidal tanks in which the water rises and falls for inter-tidal fauna. In other tanks, glass dividing panels give the impression that predator fish and their prey are swimming together. The Dolphinarium is unusually far from the sea, and obtaining warm salt water is a problem, so "sea water" is artificially prepared and the temperature kept at about 70 degrees Fahrenheit (21 degrees Centigrade).

There is a **mini-zoo** on the grounds which allows children to meet raccoons, rabbits, frogs and turtles.

Since the zoo is hemmed in by the city and has no space to expand, it has a second section outside Antwerp. The **Planckendael Domain**, at Leuvensesteenweg 582, open 9am-4:45 or 9am-6:30pm, depending on the season, is an old country residence near Malines, which can be reached by Bus 25 (the bus stop is directly in front of the entrance) or by train (alight at the Malines station).

Most of the animals live in spacious areas among the trees and shrubs, and visitors can stroll along pleasant paths to observe them. This is where the zoo carries out its breeding program. The park provides an excellent place for the animals to rear their young.

Cogels-Osylei – A Different Side of Antwerp

Cogels-Osylei is situated behind the railroad tracks in the Zurenbourg Quarter of what used to be the town of Berchem. Antwerp incorporated its smaller neighbors, including Berchem, into the city. Berchem was a neighborhood of such ostentatious eccentricity that dedicated preservationists waged a 15-year battle to save it from "development".

Some 400 houses on 10 streets, radiate extravagance-without-taste so charmingly that this has become a chic neighborhood.

A building in Cogels-Osylei

The neighborhood was built at the turn of this century, and the 16 architects who created it were certainly pandering to the pretentiousness of would-be-rich owners. There are splashes of art nouveau and art deco, but most of the styles are unidentifiable.

However it is fun, and certainly worth a visit. The house at 2 Generaal Capiaumontstraat, now a restaurant, boasts a tower and a free-standing column where a Muse perches, playing a pair of trumpets and the house at 11 Waterloostraat is embellished with a mosaic of the Battle of Waterloo. Wander the streets and discover the strange allegorical figures, birds and beasts that delighted the builders. Antwerpians have a delightful sense of humor.

Curious and carefree monkeys at the Antwerp Zoo

"MUSTS" IN ANTWERP

For those of you who have a limited time in Antwerp and are not sure what to see, we have listed a few of the nicest sites.

Grote Markt and Stadhuis (Town Hall): The central market place, dominated by the Renaissance style Stadhuis, the Brabo fountain, and the restored guild houses. Stadhuis is at Grote Markt 1. Tel. 220.82.11. Open Mon.-Wed., Fri. 9am-3pm. Sat. noon-4pm. Closed Sundays and public holidays (see "The Flavor of Old Antwerp – Around Grote Markt and the Cathedral").

The Cathedral: The largest Gothic church in Belgium, with works by Rubens and other artists inside. Handschoenmarkt near Grote Markt. Tel. 231.30.33. Open Mon.-Fri. 10am-5pm. Sat. and eve of church holidays 10am-3pm. Sun. and church holidays 1pm-4pm (see "The Flavor of Old Antwerp – Around Grote Markt and the Cathedral").

Plantin-Moretus Museum: The history of printing in the former house of the premier

The gardens at Rubens' House

printing family in Europe. Vrijdag Markt 22. Tel. 233.02.94, fax 226.25.16. Open Tues.-Sun. 10am-5pm. Closed public holidays (see "From the Cathedral to the Printing Museum").

Rubens' House: Home of Peter Paul Rubens, the most outstanding and influential artist in 17th century Flanders. Wappersstraat 9-11. Tel. 232.47.47. Open daily 10am-5pm. Closed public holidays (see "Glimpse of a Golden Age – Grote Markt to Rubens' House").

Museum voor Schone Kunsten (Fine Arts): Exceptional collection spanning five centuries, emphasis on Flemish and Belgian artists. Leopold de Waelplaats. Tel. 238.78.09. Open daily 10am-5pm, except Monday. Closed public holidays. Free entry (see "Other Sites").

St. Paul's Church: Late Gothic style, with baroque additions, especially inside. Rich art collection including works by Flemish Masters. Paulusstraat 20-22. Tel. 232.32.67. Open May-September 2-5pm; October-April 9am-noon. Closed Sun.-Mon. Free entry (see "The Flavor of Old Antwerp – Around Grote Markt and the Cathedral").

The Steen: An ancient castle, containing the Archeological Museum and National Maritime Museum. On the waterfront not far from Grote Markt. Steenplein 1. Tel. 232.08.50. Open daily 10am-5pm. Closed Mon., holidays, Jan. 1-2, May 1, Nov. 1-2, Dec. 25-26 (see "The Flavor of Old Antwerp – Around Grote Markt and the Cathedral").

The Zoo and Museum of Natural History: A world famous zoo with many rare animals. Koningin Astridplein 26. Tel. 231.16.40. Open daily 9am-6pm in summer, till 5pm in winter (see "Other Sites").

The rich interior of St. Paul's Church

MAKING THE MOST OF YOUR STAY

Wining and Dining

Antwerpians like to wine and dine, and the city has some local specialties. Seafood, especially bottomless pots of steamed mussels, is a superb choice in Antwerp. Eels, too, are a favorite – especially cooked in green sauce (*paling in 't groen*). Other specialities are chicken, rabbit, chicory and strawberries.

Waterzoi, the thick white stew of Belgium, has its own interpretation here. And, of course, there are always *frites* (fried potatoes).

Antwerp "hands" are sold as butter cookies or as chocolates, and the famous Belgian chocolate makers have outlets all over town.

Restaurants

Antwerp has hundreds of restaurants including all classes, prices and types of cuisine. The following are some of the best. Prices given are per person. Drinks are extra.

CRÈME DE LA CRÈME

La Pérouse: Steenplein. Tel. 231.31.51. Open Sept. 30 to end of May, except Monday and holidays. French cuisine.

Sir Anthony Van Dijck: Oude Koornmarkt 16, Vlaeykensgang. Tel. 233.91.25. Closed Saturday and Sunday, April 20-27 and most of August. Nouvelle cuisine.

't Fornuis: Reyndersstraat 24. Tel. 233.62.70. Closed

Saturday, Sunday and most of August. Nouvelle cuisine.

Vateli: Kipdorpvest 50. Tel. 238.87.25. Closed Sunday, Monday, holidays and July. French and regional specialities.

DELUXE RESTAURANTS

De Lepeleer: Lange St.-Annastraat 8-10. Tel. 225.19.31. Closed Saturday noon, Sunday, holidays and most of August. French, nouvelle cuisine and fish.

Den Gulden Greffoen: Hoogstraat 37. Tel. 231.50.46. Closed Saturday noon, Sunday, holidays, most of July.

La Rade: Van Dijckkaai 8. Tel. 233.37.37. Closed Saturday noon, Sunday, early March and most of July. French, traditional and Flemish specialities.

Machtans: Tolstraat 70. Tel. 237.86.93. Closed Saturday and Sunday noon, Monday, Thursday and July.

VERY GOOD RESTAURANTS

De Twee Atheners: Vlasmarkt 25-27. Tel. 231.34.61. Closed Wednesday and September. Greek food.

Koperen Ketel: Wiegstraat 5. Tel. 233.12.74. Closed Saturday noon, Sunday, Monday noon and most of August. French and traditional cuisine.

La Moule Parqúee: Wapenstraat 18. Tel. 238.49.08. Closed Monday, Saturday noon and most of May.

Manoir: Everdijstraat 13. Tel. 232.76.97. Closed Wednesday and mid-July to mid-August. French cuisine.

Panache: Statiestraat 17. Tel. 232.69.05. Closed end July to end August. French, traditional and grills.

Peerdestal: Wijngaardstraat 8-10. Tel. 231.95.03. This

Beautiful decor at a bar-restaurant at the Centraal Station

renovated horse stable makes a specialty of horse steaks – surprisingly good. Also French, traditional and seafood.

In de Schaduw van de Kathedral: Handschoenmarkt 17. Tel. 232.40.14. Closed Monday, Tuesday and early-May. Specializes in seafood.

Stoofpot: Schuttershefstraat 37. Tel. 234.39.31. Popular with young people. Reservations recommended. Open from 5pm weekdays, and also for lunch on weekends.

Willy: Generaal Lemanstraat 54, Berchem. Tel. 218.88.07. Closed July.

Beer Cafés

Beer, a serious drink throughout Belgium, is greatly appreciated in Antwerp. It has many beer cafés which specialize in huge selections, traditional decor and knowledgeable staff to help you make the right choice – nothing is worse than a heavy sweet beer when you need a pick-me-up, and nothing is better for a good night's sleep than a dark trappist beer.

Most beer cafés have a substantial selection, including "table" pilsners, a few imports and cherry, abbey and lambic beer, but the special houses have even more.

Just on the edge of Antwerp stands the city's brewery, **De Koninck**, which was founded

in 1833. The brewery is small, selling mainly in the city and its surroundings. It makes just one beer, a racy amber brew that should be drunk young and cool. About 80 percent of the pubs in Antwerp sell De Koninck, and they serve it in a round, stemmed, hand-blown glass, called a *Bolleke*. That means "small ball" and many fans of the brew order their beer by the name of the glass and won't drink it out of any other kind. Tradition is important, and the firm still uses slim brown bottles embossed with the Antwerp Hand.

Across the street from the brewery is the brewery pub. Here elderly regulars order a tiny glass of *geist* – the ferment skimmed off as beer brews. It is a thick, brown, cloudy liquid, containing little alcohol, but said to aid the digestion. It tastes awful.

There are some 2500 beer cafés to choose from in Antwerp (see "Entertainment"), and the following are just a few of the most highly recommended:

De Boer van Tienen:

Mechelseplein 6. Open daily from 9am, closed Sunday at 8pm. One of the best examples of a "typical" Antwerp café. Tel. 233.04.24.

Herberg Den Artist: Museumstraat 45. Tel. 238.09.95. Open Thurs.-Fri. from noon, Sat.-Sun. from 4pm. Kitchen open until 2am. One of the top cafés, with an art nouveau interior and 500 kinds of beer.

De Groote witte Arend: Reynderstraat 12-18. Tel. 232.08.80. Open 11am to 1 or 2am weekdays, to 3am on weekends. A large wine list, classical music exhibitions.

De Vagant: Reyndersstraat 25. Tel. 233.15.38 Open weekdays from 11 am, and weekends from 1pm. Classical music and beer, but the thing to explore here is the *genever* (gin) selection.

Het Grote Ongenoegen: Jeruzalemstraat 9. Open 5pm-3am weekdays, 2pm-4am weekends, and Sundays to 2pm. More than 1200 kinds of beer from 35 countries. This café is in the Guiness Book of Records for having the largest selection of beer in the world.

Kulminator: Vleminckveld 32-34. Tel. 232.45.38. Open Tues.-Fri. 11am-1am, open Mon. at 8:15pm, and Sat. at 5pm, closed Sunday and holidays. One of the most popular beer cafés, which stocks about 500 beers, listed on a 24-page menu. Classical music and dark wood give the interior atmosphere.

Riverside Jazz Club: Paulusstraat st 23. Open Wed.-Sun. from 8pm. Top jazz musicians perform here.

Entertainment

The tourist office publishes an entertainment listing, *Kalendar Antwerpen*, telling what's on at the theaters, concert halls and puppet theaters. The tourist office or your hotel can help you make a choice and book the tickets, since it is the Antwerp custom to pick up tickets directly at the theater. You can get information and make bookings at Theatercentrum, Theaterplein. Tel. 234.21.46. or at Theaterwinkel, St. Jacobsmarkt 74. Tel. 233.71.60.

There are several concert series and performances of classical music, opera, ballet, jazz and rock in Antwerp. The *Queen Elisabeth Hall* (Kon-Astridplein 23-24, Tel. 231.07.50) has over 2000 seats and the Concert Hall *de Singel* (Desguinlei 25, Tel. 248.38.00) has 3 halls. *Hof te Lo* is the venue for rock music. Every Monday evening, from mid-June to mid-September there are carillon concerts from the Cathedral tower, and for many people this is the time for an evening out, and the cafés and squares are full of people.

The city has about 50 movie theaters, many near the Centraal Station. Showings start about noon and films are shown in their original languages. Flemish TV shows movies and interviews in the original language.

Antwerp has plenty of bars and clubs befitting a port city. The cabarets, discos and sex clubs change fairly often; ask the advice of the concierge.

The best-known entertainment centers are:

Groenplaats and Grote Markt: with famous Antwerp café terraces.

High Town: Hoogstraat, Pelgrimstraat, Pieter Potstraat and surroundings. "Brown" pubs, bistros, jazz-clubs etc. "Brown" pubs are old and the walls have been stained by cigarette smoke over the years. They are generally dark, with low ceilings and an intimate atmosphere.

Stadswaag: Jazz, punk music, beer cellars.

De Keyserlei: Taverns, boulevard-cafés and many terraces.

Neighbourhood of Centraal Station: Statiestraat, Gemeentestraat, De Conscienceplein. Discothèques, nightclubs, gay-bars.

Riverside Quarter: Sailors' pubs, the red-light district.

Quartier Latin: Near the City Theater. Artists' cafés and bars.

Festivals

All the year round there are a great many traditional or folklore events, here are just a few:

International Film Festival: Special attention is given to non-commercial films. January-February.

A night scene in Grote Markt

The Antwerp Jumping: International horse jumping (and goose riding) contest. Beginning of March.

Sword-dancing: A custom dating from the Middle Ages. Mid-Lent in front of the Cathedral.

Evening Walks during the Summer: In the center of the Old Town on Monday and Saturday evenings. May-September.

Carillon Concerts: From the Cathedral tower on Monday evenings, from mid-June to mid-September. Also July-August, on Sun. evenings. For many people it is their evening out.

World Folklore Festival: Folklore groups from all over the world create a lively show at Schoten. July.

'Steen' Festival: Theater, jazz, dance, poetry and more. July - August. (Odd numbered years).

Biennial for Sculpture: Every two years, a large open-air exhibition, during the summer.

Antwerp Holiday Week: A variety of festivities including the Ommegang pageant, the Rubens Market, guided walks, carillon concerts. Mid-August.

Middelheim Jazz Festival: For a whole week, old and contem-

porary jazz music. Mid-August. (Odd numbered years).

Edegem International Folk-dance Festival: International folk-dance groups. Mid-August. There are similar Festivals in July and September.

September Festivities: Festivities are organized all over town, with guild celebrations, giants' parade, Theater Market, fire works, and more.

The Antwerp Tattoo: Grote Markt. Square. A selection of military bands (afternoons) and tattoo (evenings). Beginning of September.

The Antwerp Marathon: A sporting event popular with athletes and spectators alike. In the district of Berchem. September.

European Community Championship: Tennis tournament with the world's top players. The Sportpaleis (Schijnpoortweg 113). November.

Filling the Basket: Where to Shop and for What

Belgian-made goods take pride of place in Antwerp, and there is a tremendous selection. The range is not quite as great as that in Brussels, but the city is more tranquil and the shops less crowded, so many people prefer to do their shopping in Antwerp.

Luxury Shops

Antwerp has many shopping centers, boutiques and specialty shops. Well-known streets for elegant and expensive shopping are **Meir**, **De Keyserlei** and **Leysstraat**. Meir has many department stores,

and also boutiques selling high quality fashions, such as *Hey* which caters to young people, and has branches in Brussels. De Keyserlei has many theaters and cinemas as well as stylish shops. Eiermarkt and Schoenmarkt are another two streets with elegant and expensive shops.

Chic and expensive *galleries* are found at *Patio Meir* on the Meir and *Nieuwe Gaanderij* on Huidevettersstraat. The *Empire Shopping Center*, and *Centure* near the Centraal Station are not bad places to shop.

The main pedestrian malls, where you can stroll, undisturbed by traffic, are around the beautiful **Groenplaats**, **Hoogstraat** and **Offerandestraat**. The area near the Grote Markt has many small shops, and the area between Suikerrui and Vlasmarkt Reyndersstraat includes small shops, cafés, restaurants and fast food outlets.

Department stores are also abundant, for those who want to shop in more standard moderately priced stores. *Bazaar* on the Meir is the biggest department store, but Antwerp also has *C&A*, *Marks and Spencer* and *Innovation*, better known as "Inno".

DIAMONDS

Antwerp is home to the most important diamond industry in the world, 60 percent of all diamonds are polished and traded here every year. The Antwerp diamond district was traditionally closed to the public, but recently has become more open. Visitors can now watch craftsmen at work and can learn the meaning of color, clarity, cut, carat, certification, fluorescence and valuation. Remember to bring your passport to get a tax exemption if you wish to buy anything.

Diamondland: Appelmansstraat 33a. Tel. 234.36.12. fax. 233.58.44. Open Mon.-Sat. 9am-6pm. Visitors receive an explanation as well as a chance to look at the showroom.

Van Moppes: Maarschalk Gerardstraat 2. Tel. 233.77.67. Open until 5:30pm. Also has explanations for visitors and a showroom.

Ruys: Jorespoort 26. A gorgeous Art Nouveau store.

Dilady (Provincial Diamond Museum): 31-33 Lange Herentalsestraat. Tel. 231.86.45. Open daily 10am-5pm.

Steigrad (Diamond Council): Hoveniersstraat 22. Tel. 222.05.11. Open Mon.-Fri. 10am-12pm.

Moderately Priced Shops

Lace: Lace shops are scattered around town, with a large concentration in the vicinity of the Cathedral. There is a fine lace shop, *Dupon Kant*, across from Rubens' house.

Chocolates: *Godiva* and *Léonidas* chocolates are easy to find, but there are local shops, too, such as *Del Rey* at Appelmansstraat 5, *Suikerjan* at St. Jacobsmarkt 42, *H. Burie* at Gasthuisstraat 3 and *Goossens* at Isabellalei 6.

Toy shops: Include *Christiaensen*, Huidevettersstraat 12; *Herman Verschooten*, Kammenstraat 46 and Eiermarkt 14, and *Bouripoef* (dozens of stuffed toys) at St. Jorispoort 19.

Cigars: A specialist in Havana cigars is *Frans van de Voorde*, Lange Koepoorstraat 43-49.

Old books: These are displayed along the **Hoogstraat**, or try *De Slegte*, at Meir 40, *De Witte Sinjoor* at Melkmarkt 12, *Moorthamers* at Wapper 5 and *Oude Borze*, at Oude Beurs 62. Almost all the book stores have English-language books and there is a good selection at *Veritas*, Huidevettersstraat 21, and at *Standaard Boekhandel*, at No. 55 on the same street.

Hunting and sports weapons: These can be found at *Lang & Zn.*, Lombardenvest 8, and *Reymen*, Koningen Astridplein 37.

Hunting clothes: Can be found at *E. Kettner*, Antwerpsestraat 31 in Mortsel. Horse riders can find all their requirements at *Stoeterij't Ros Beyaert*, Steenhouwersvest 18.

Nautical goods: Antwerp is the place for nautical goods. *The Antwerpse Lloyd Bookshop* on the Eiermarkt has an outstanding selection of nautical books.

Stamps and coins: Collectors will like *Antwerp Stamp Center*, Lange Nieuwstraat 104; *De Beul* down the street at No. 113-117; *Roels*, St. Katelijnevest 45 and *Raassens* at No. 34; and *Campo Rodan*, Oude Vaartplaats 55.

For a unique shopping experience, take a look at the stores in **Little Russia**, the area around the Falconplein, which caters especially to Russian seamen. **Little Greece**, in the area of St. Paul's Church sells Greek specialities.

Markets

The main market area is around Grote Markt. A special event takes place here annually on **August 15**, during a week-long celebration, when vendors dress up in 17th-century costume and set up their stalls in the **Grote Markt** and surrounding streets. Prizes are given for the best booths, and the vendors are never too busy to smile for the camera. It's quite a lot of fun to watch a man in velvet and a ruff demonstrating the latest thing in vacuum cleaners.

The Bird Market: Oude Vaartplaats, near the City Theater. Every Sunday morning 9am-1pm. This sprawling market includes much, much more than birds. It is really a general market, where you can buy flowers, live animals, plants, textiles, antiques or foodstuffs.

The Friday Market: Vrijdagmarkt, facing the Plantin-Moretus Museum. Every

Diamonds galore

Wednesday and Friday 9am-12pm. An auction of old furniture and second-hand goods.

The Open-Air Workshop: On the Wapper. Every Saturday from April to September. This workshop is set up for artists to work and to show their work.

The Antiques Market: Lijnwaadmarkt, near the Cathedral. Every Saturday from Easter to October, 9am-3pm.

Quite often, the merchants on a particular street get together for a *braderij*, a sidewalk sale. In fact, there is a street called Braderijstraat leading off the Grote Markt, and the shops in that area often set up such sales. They follow no set schedule.

Important Addresses and Phone Numbers

Police: Tel. 101.
Medical emergency: Tel. 900.
Ambulance: Tel. 100.
Anti-Poison Center: Tel. 345.45.45.
Sabena: Tel. 511.90.30.; 231.68.25.
Airport Information Deurne: Tel. 239.59.60.
Centraal Railway Station: Tel. 233.39.15.
City Tourist Office: Tel. 232.01.03, fax. 231.19.37 (Grote Markt 15).
Municipal Sport Service: Tel. 220.86.75. (Grote Markt 5).
Information on theaters, concerts, galleries; reservations: *EKU*: Nationalestraat 5. Tel. 233.71.60.
Theatercentrum: Italiëlei 112. Tel. 234.21.46.

CONSULATES

U.S.A.: Nationalestraat 5. Tel. 232.18.00.
Great Britain: Lange Klarenstraat 24. Tel. 232.69.40.
Ireland: Rudolfstraat 30. Tel. 237.69.94.

Ghent and Bruges

From both Brussels and Antwerp you can easily visit two charming Middle Age cities: Ghent and Bruges.

Ghent (Gent)

This city, 40 miles from Antwerp, is the capital of Eastern Flanders – a university town and second harbour of Belgium. It is also an important textile and industrial center. It is called "the city of the Flowers" because horticulture is one of its specialties. Every five years the Floral Palace welcomes the Ghent Flower Show (1990, 1995 etc.).

Ghent Tourist Office on Belfortstraat 9 (TEL 25.36.41) will be able to tell you about the different conducted tours as well as boat-trips. Tours of Ghent are centered on the Old City, which you shouldn't miss visiting at night. The illuminations (every evening from 8pm from Easter to October) make the walk unforgettable.

St. Baafs Kathedraal (St-Bavon Cathedral – open from Apr. till Sept. 9:30-12am and 2-6pm, Sun. 1-6pm, from Oct. till March 10:30-12am and 2:30-4pm, Sun. 2-5pm) is worth a visit especially because of the famous altarpiece of the *Adoration of the Mystic Lamb*, attributed to the painter Jan Van

A serene boat-trip in Ghent

A Cathedral at Ghent

Eyck and to his brother Hubert.

This altarpiece is exhibited in one of the 20 chapels of the Cathedral. Since its solemn installation in 1432, it has known quite a number of traumas. The protestants wanted to burn it, it was relieved of a number of its panels, it was exhibited in Paris then in Berlin, it was copied, stolen, and then found by the Americans and eventually taken back to its place in the Cathedral.

This extraordinary piece of art is composed of 248 characters and more than 40 different plants and flowers in luminous colors.

Not far away from the Cathedral are the **Belfry** and the **Drapery Hall**. The Belfry was built in 1321 and 1380. It went through numerous transformations before assuming its present form which dates from 1913.

The imposing 300-ft, high work of art is dominated by a copper dragon which symbolizes the power of the guilds of Ghent.

In the Drapery Hall, at the side of the Belfry, an audio-visual show on the city of Ghent is presented every day except Monday. The **Stadhuis** (City Hall) is built in Gothic and Renaissance styles. The construction was begun in 1518, interrupted for almost 20 years and restarted in 1595.

From the City Hall, taking the left, one reaches St. Nicolas church and then St. Michel bridge. From here, one has a beautiful view of the Belfry, the cathedral, and further away, of the **Gravensteen** (Castle of the counts of Flanders, which can be visited every day except Mondays, 9am-5:15pm from Apr. until Sept and 9am-3:15pm from Jan. until March).

From the St. Michel Bridge, go down the stairs which lead to the **Graslei** (the "herb quay") and to the **Koornlei** (the wheat quay). From here, you'll be able to admire the wonderful facades of the Guild houses on the banks of the river Lys.

Two museums in Ghent deserve a special visit: the Fine Arts Museum (Museum voor Schone Kunsten) and the Bijloke Museum. The **Fine Arts Museum** is situated on the edge of the park of the Citadel, where the Floral Palace can be found (open 9-12:30am and 1:20-5:30pm, closed on Sundays Feb.-Sept., and on Sundays-Mondays Oct.-Jan. It is also closed on Bank holidays). It possesses vast collections of Flemish and contemporary art.

The Bijloke Museum (same hours as the Fine Art Museum) houses an archeology museum as well as sumptuous decorative arts collections.

Bruges (Brugge)

Bruges "the Beautiful" is situated on Northern Flanders, 30 miles from Ghent. It is crossed by the Reye and cut by numerous canals. The tourist office in the Grand-Place (open in summer 9am-8pm and in winter 9am-5:45pm, closed on Sundays during winter. Tel. 33.07.11) will inform you about organised tours, boat excursions on canals, and also about horse-drawn carriage tours through the city. You can buy a reduced price ticket for the four big Bruges museums.

Have a walk in Bruges' streets. In the evening the street lights

The City Hall at Ghent, built in Gothic and Renaissance styles

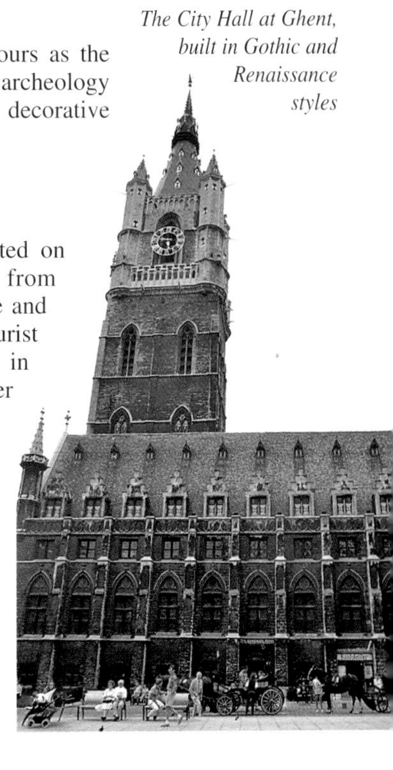

Touring Bruges

(from May until September) give an extraordinary effect to the Middle Age Buildings.

Start your walk at the Grand' Place which is surrounded by beautiful gabled houses. It is looked down on by the Belfry, which at 200ft. is the highest in Belgium. If you go to admire the Guild houses at 2pm you'll be able to hear the sound of the 47 bells of the carillon (Concerts: Wed. Sat. Sun.).

Walk through Breidelstraat and you'll reach the Bourg Square framed by the Basilic of Holy Blood, the City Hall in flamboyant Gothic style, the ancient Renaissance Court Office and the Palace of Justice.

Bruges is famous for its museums and numerous Flemish painters. It was in this city that Van Eyck and Memling, two great Masters of the Flemish School lived (see "Art").

The Stedelijk Museum (Groeninge Museum) is open every day (except on Tuesdays) 9:30am-6:30pm, and from Oct.-March 9:30am-12pm and 2pm-6pm). It holds extraordinary art works of Van Eyck, Van der Goes, and Memling. The latter was to Bruges what Brueghel was to Brussels. He painted very calm and severe portraits. Contemporary Belgian Art with Delvaux and Magritte is well represented.

The Memling Museum, situated in the ancient St. Jean Hospital, is the second biggest museum where the works of the master of the portrait are exhibited. Among others is *St. Ursula's shrine*. Open Apr.-

Sept. 9am-12:30pm and 2-6pm, from Oct.-March 10am-12pm and 2-5pm, closed on Wed.

Also worth a visit is the **Brangwin Museum** which possesses a very beautiful collection of art objects and ancient sketches of Bruges and the **Gruuthuse Museum** of decorative arts (both have same opening hours as the Stedelijk Museum).

The Kantcentrum (Center of lace work) is an interesting place to visit (open from 2-6pm every day and on Wed. and Sat. 2-4pm). There you'll discover the delicate art of lace on a bobbin.

INDEX

QUESTIONNAIRE

In our efforts to keep up with the pace and pulse of Brussels and Antwerp, we kindly ask your cooperation in sharing with us any information which you may have as well as your comments. We would greatly appreciate your completing and returning of the following questionnaire. Feel free to add additional pages.

Our many thanks!

To: Inbal Travel Information (1983) Ltd.
18 Hayetzira st.
Ramat Gan 52521
Israel

Name: ______________________________

Address: ______________________________

Occupation: ______________________________

Date of visit: ______________________________

____

Purpose of trip (vacation, business, etc.): ______________

____

Comments/Information: ______________________________

____

____

____

____

____

____

____

3/95

INBAL Travel Information Ltd.
P.O.B 1870 Ramat Gan
ISRAEL 52117